DORIS DAY

D0071558

DORIS DAY

A Pyramid Illustrated History of the Movies

by
GEORGE MORRIS

General Editor: **TED SENNETT**

PUBLICATIONS

For my parents, G.C. and Dorothy

DORIS DAY
A Pyramid Illustrated History of the Movies

Copyright © 1976 by Pyramid Communications, Inc.

All rights reserved. No part of this publication may be reproduced or transmitted in any form or by any means, electronic or mechanical, including photocopy, recording, or any information storage and retrieval system, without permission in writing from the publisher.

Pyramid edition published February 1976

ISBN 0-515-03959-4

Library of Congress Catalog Card Number: 75-42514

Printed in the United States of America

Pyramid Books are published by Pyramid Communications, Inc. Its trademarks, consisting of the word "Pyramid" and the portrayal of a pyramid, are registered in the United States Patent Office.

Pyramid Communications, Inc., 919 Third Avenue, New York, N.Y. 10022

(graphic design by anthony basile)

ACKNOWLEDGMENTS

I would like to express my gratitude to the following people who assisted me in the preparation of this book:

William Dolive; Molly Haskell; Doug Lemza of Films Incorporated; Howard Mandelbaum; Roger McNiven; my editor Ted Sennett; Patrick Sheehan and Joseph Balian of the Library of Congress Motion Picture Section; Charles Silver in the Museum of Modern Art Department of Film; Mike Stevens and Joseph Seechack of Metromedia Television, New York City; and for his unending patience and enthusiasm, Jim Stark.

Photographs: Jerry Vermilye, Cinemabilia, and the companies that produced and distributed the films of Doris Day: Warner Brothers, Universal Pictures, Metro-Goldwyn-Mayer, Twentieth Century-Fox, Paramount Pictures, Arwin Films

CONTENTS

Doris Day was the most successful female star to emerge during the post-war years. Her name consistently spelled box-office magic for almost twenty years, she was the leading moneymaker for Columbia Records during most of the fifties, and in 1968 she embarked on a television series which ranked among the top six in the national Nielsen ratings within weeks of its debut, never wavering too far from the top twenty shows on the air thereafter.

In an industry where the lifespan of women stars is noticeably shorter than that of their male counterparts, Day's longevity is even more remarkable. She was a star in her first film in 1948, and she stayed a star until her last film (to date) in 1968. Eleven of her thirty-nine films are among the largest-grossing motion pictures of all time. By the end of 1951 (her third year in films), Betty Grable was her only feminine rival at the box-office. In 1952, when the *Motion Picture Herald* announced its annual poll of the top ten film stars, Doris Day had unequivocally assumed the top position. Her popularity remained fairly steady throughout the decade until 1959, the year that *Pillow Talk* was released. From 1959 to 1966, an unparalleled period of seven years, Doris Day dominated the top ten polls. During four of those years, she actually *was* the number one box-office draw in the

INTRODUCTION: THE STAR NEXT DOOR

United States.

Doris Day's initial success with the moviegoing public is much easier to understand than the length and intensity of her overall career. Her duration as a star over a period of two decades assumes the aspect of a sociological phenomenon. There were better singers, better comediennes, and certainly better actresses. But, as Molly Haskell has astutely pointed out in *From Reverence to Rape*, there is something in the persona of Doris Day—unlike other female stars of her era, e.g., Marilyn Monroe, Elizabeth Taylor, Grace Kelly, and Audrey Hepburn—that coincides with the American image of womanhood far more accurately than most men, or women, would admit.

For instance, Doris Day was one of the few women in films who did not seek to define herself in the mirror reflection of a man's fantasies or desires. Her chauvinistic exuberance was aimed at getting ahead, not getting a man. Day's image contradicts itself throughout her screen roles. She did a remarkably intricate piece of tightrope-walking between buoyant energy and determined ambition, between

LOVE ME OR LEAVE ME (1955). As Ruth Etting

sunny optimism and stubborn self-reliance. Indeed, in many of Day's performances, it is difficult to tell where one leaves off and the other begins.

Therefore, Day's screen persona is infinitely more complex than the tired jokes about virginity, filters, and "Goody Two-Shoes" would suggest. If one bothers to put the films—and her characters *in* the films—under close scrutiny, one of the most fascinating women in the history of films begins to emerge.

Doris Day's career in films is sharply divided into three distinct periods. From 1948 to 1954, the period she was under exclusive contract to Warner Bros., Day made a series of highly forgettable, unimaginative musicals in which she was alternately cast as tomboys and devoted wives, ingenues and career-minded singers. Her most exciting and challenging performances fall in the middle period, a relatively brief span of time (1955-1957) which encompasses the three best roles of her career: Ruth Etting in *Love Me or Leave Me*, Jo McKenna in *The Man Who Knew Too Much*, and Babe Williams in *Pajama Game*. The last and most successful cycle comprises the chain of sex comedies initiated by producer Ross Hunter and writer Stanley Shapiro in 1959 with *Pillow Talk*. It is during this latter phase that Day's very real comedic talents ossified and congealed. Audiences seemed willing to go on forever watching Rock Hudson melt Day's frigidity, while she alternately condemned his promiscuity and questioned his masculinity. The formula worked repeatedly, and so Day's thespic abilities were never stretched, never allowed to expand or grow beyond the endless stream of puerile farces which emanated from the studios' assembly lines throughout the sixties.

Once the Shapiro syndrome was implanted in the public's favor, any deviation from the norm was met with stony disapproval from the exhibitors and non-attendance by her fans. Movies like *Billy Rose's Jumbo* and *The Ballad of Josie*, in which Day accepts her age and rings some of the subtler changes on her persona, were abysmal failures at the box office.

Nevertheless, as separate as these three divisions in Day's career seem, there are instances within each period in which contradictions and modifications surface. The unifying constant, of course, is the fact that she remained indisputably a star of the highest caliber. It is a testament to Day's resilience—and to the astute judgment of her late agent-husband Martin Melcher—that she had the opportunity to recharge her career so often, and succeeded.

The fact that Day is genuinely talented is often obscured by the

enormity of her popularity and her petrified public image toward the end of her film career. Day's mellow singing style is redolent of the forties. Like many singers who emerged in the big band era, her voice blended into the overall texture of the orchestras with which she sang. Day's vocal delivery in her early films is very subdued. The virtual lack of any dynamics or dramatic phrasing reveals the years in which her voice was used primarily as a complementary instrument aimed at achieving that big band sound.

A change in Day's vocal style parallels her rise in movies. Her singing becomes more self-assured. Rather than merely supplementing the songs and their lyrics, her voice begins to implement and dominate them. Her appreciation for the contours of a melody, and her sensitivity to the phrasing of a lyric grow with each film in the fifties. By the time she made her best musicals (*Calamity Jane*, *Love Me or Leave Me*, *Pajama Game*, and *Billy Rose's Jumbo*) Day had developed into the best musical actress in movies. Her ability to delineate character and express emotion in the context of a musical number was unrivaled as the decade came to a close.

Unfortunately for Day, however, her control and mastery of musical comedy performance coincided with the death of the musical

as a viable genre. In order to survive, she turned to straight dramatic parts, and eventually to the sex comedies.

As a dramatic actress, Day was as good as her material and her director allowed her to be. Under Alfred Hitchcock (*The Man Who Knew Too Much*), she gave the finest performance of her career. Under David Miller (*Midnight Lace*), she undeniably gave her worst. Day rarely had the opportunity to work with good directors. Hitchcock was an isolated instance. She occasionally got a director of wit and imagination such as Stanley Donen and Frank Tashlin, or even an accomplished craftsman on the order of Michael Curtiz or Richard Quine, but more often she was stuck with hacks like Michael Gordon and Ralph Levy.

While she always met the challenge of difficult roles and acquitted herself admirably in them, Doris Day seemed unable to invest her more ordinary vehicles with dimensions and resonances absent in the script and direction. She lacked the inner resources that the best actors have which would have enabled her to transcend the most mindless material. It would have been fascinating to see her tackle the Anne Bancroft role in *The Graduate* or the Ellen Burstyn role in *Alice Doesn't Live Here Anymore*, parts which would have tested and extended her range in a manner that might have kept her going well into the seventies.

Day's reluctance to play older women, and her aversion to the new permissiveness in contemporary films, circumscribed her career. The considerable technical resources at Hollywood's disposal could not keep Doris Day young forever. Her inability to adapt and change became painful to watch toward the end of the sixties, though interestingly enough, she herself allows director Frank Tashlin to satirize this element of her persona in *Caprice*, a movie in which the star uncomfortably resembles a mannequin.

Even under Tashlin, however, Day's forthright individuality and athletic stamina are never completely submerged. A direct honesty shines through most of her performances that connected with audiences immediately. Her no-nonsense approach to life may not have been the stuff that sexual fantasies are made of, but she *was* sexy in a healthy, open way. She got out and worked in the daytime, but one could believe that she found time for nocturnal pleasures as well. She taught night school, headed a labor committee, bred lobsters, and chased potential advertising accounts; but she never denied herself a love life when the opportunity presented itself. In this respect she is one of the few independent women in postwar cinema. She did not exist to be adored by men; she existed for herself, and continued to create—and recreate—herself in a manner which strengthens Molly Haskell's contention that Doris Day was "a home-grown existential female lifted into the modern world."

Doris von Kappelhoff was born April 3, 1924 in Cincinnati, Ohio, the second child and only daughter of Alma Sophia and Frederick Wilhelm von Kappelhoff. Her mother named her after her favorite actress, Doris Kenyon, and there is a covert hint running through many of Day's "official" biographies that Alma Sophia may have been a minor-league version of Gypsy Rose Lee's aggressive Mama Rose. Kappelhoff *père* was a church organist, choirmaster, and teacher of violin and piano who instilled a love and appreciation of music in his daughter.

When Doris was twelve, her German-Catholic parents separated and she went with her mother and older brother Paul to live in Evanston, a suburb of Cincinnati. Encouraging Doris to take dancing lessons, Alma worked in a local bakery to support her small family. Soon, Doris was entertaining at amateur events all over Cincinnati. She teamed up with an adolescent tap dancer, Jerry Doherty, and as Doherty and Kappelhoff, these teenage threats to Astaire and Rogers copped a $500 prize in a contest run by a local department store.

The euphoria at winning such a sum of money convinced the mothers of both teenagers that their fledglings were ready for the big time. The Kappelhoffs and the Dohertys migrated to California,

where Doris and Jerry studied under Louis DaPron, a prominent instructor of tap dance. The move proved unwise in the long run, however, as they won few professional engagements. Both Mrs. Kappelhoff and Mrs. Doherty were forced to do part-time work to keep the tap lessons going, the stomachs full, and the rent paid.

Ending their hiatus in California, the disillusioned little band returned to Cincinnati where Doris and Jerry landed a job dancing with the touring Fanchon and Marco stage show. Before the two families could return to California, however, Day's right leg was seriously injured in an automobile crash in Hamilton, Ohio. This tragic accident curtailed her dancing career, confining the young girl to hospitals for fourteen months.

Day's mother was determined to get the child into the limelight. Temporarily stymied by the auto accident, Alma began to channel her dreams of Doris the dancer into Doris the singer. As soon as Doris had convalesced, Alma began taking in sewing in order to pay for the girl's singing lessons with Grace Raine, the teacher to whom the star has stated, in numerous interviews, she is eternally indebted. Day

As a band singer in 1947

gradually began singing on local radio shows, often without pay, in order to gain experience and technique. While singing on "Karlin's Karnival" over radio station WCPO in Cincinnati, Barney Rapp, a band leader who was opening his own night club, heard her and offered her a job at $25 a week.

There was one condition, however. The last name had to go. Taking his cue from the song "Day by Day," which Doris had sung often on "Karlin's Karnival," Rapp christened his protegée Doris Day.

Day's relaxed vocal style was very popular at Rapp's club, and her success with him escalated her career, leading to extensive tours with the bands of Fred Waring, Bob Crosby, and Les Brown. It was during this burgeoning period of her singing career that she married Al Jordan, a trombone player in Gene Krupa's band. Married in March 1941, they divorced two years later after a marriage spent mostly on the road.

Disillusioned, Day returned to Cincinnati with her year-old son Terry and moved in with her mother. After a short stint on local radio, Day entrusted the care of Terry to Alma and rejoined Les Brown for the three-year tour that was to culminate in the recording of "Sentimental Journey" and stardom.

In 1946 Day married another musician, George Weidler, the brother of MGM child actress Virginia Weidler; unfortunately, this second union also ended in divorce in 1949. The transient life style of musicians, and the difficulty of constructing a viable relationship out of buses, trailers, and hotel rooms, severely limited the singer's chances for a successful marriage at this stage of her career.

(A few years after their separation, Weidler was largely responsible for converting Day to Christian Science, a faith to which she was diligently committed until recently. Even now, she adheres to its precepts in spirit, if not to the letter.)

By the late forties Doris Day was appearing regularly on radio with such names as Bob Hope and Frank Sinatra. Her recording of "Sentimental Journey" was one of the top-selling singles of the decade. Al Levy of Century Artists Agency wangled her an interview with director Michael Curtiz, who was looking for a singer to replace the pregnant Betty Hutton in his new film. The story goes, by the apocryphal grapevine, that Day cried miserably throughout the interview; supposedly she was depressed about her impending divorce from Weidler as well as nervous about meeting the director of *Casablanca* and *Mildred Pierce*.

Whatever the details surrounding this historic confrontation, Curtiz signed her to a personal contract to star her in *Romance on the*

ROMANCE ON THE HIGH SEAS (1948). With Oscar Levant

High Seas at $500 a week. *Romance on the High Seas* was the first film Curtiz directed for Warner Bros. under a new agreement which gave the director an independent unit as well as a share in the profits of his films. Later, when the studio bought up his company, Doris Day had become its major asset.

Based on an obscure Argentine comedy, *Romance on the High Seas* was a property that had been lying around the studio for years (its original title was *Romance in High C*). Julius J. Epstein and his brother Philip, who had worked with Curtiz on such previous successes as *Four Daughters* and *Casablanca*, agreed to co-script the movie in return for the cancellation of their contract with Warner Bros.. The Epsteins' lack of enthusiasm for the project is reflected in their scenario, which veers wildly between sophisticated comedy and knockabout farce, often within the same scene.

Romance on the High Seas revolves around the efforts of a married couple (Janis Paige and Don DeFore) to gather evidence of extra-marital hanky-panky on one another. Paige plans a South Seas cruise, but has a nightclub singer (Day) impersonate her on the voyage. DeFore in turn hires a private investigator (Jack Carson) to tail his wife on the voyage, but of course, *she* has remained in New York to spy on her supposedly errant husband.

The multi-colored travel folders that accompany the credits for *Romance on the High Seas* promise a great deal of gaiety and excitement, little of which actually transpires. Curtiz' direction of this warmed-over farce is competent and nothing more. Comedy was never this director's forté, and much of the direction resembles a motley assemblage of scraps and pieces hastily patched together for a ready-made audience. Busby Berkeley receives credit for the staging of the musical sequences, but the two big "set pieces"—Avon Long's calypso-cadenced "The Tourist Trade" and the carnival finale with its explosion of balloons and streamers in a crowded ballroom—are interesting *ideas* for musical numbers that seem to have been aborted before their potential was realized.

This grab-bag package of Technicolored nonsense also features Oscar Levant milking his inferiority complex for every drop of self-disparaging humor; S. Z. "Cuddles" Sakall with his Mitteleuropa malapropisms; and such luminaries as Eric Blore and Franklin Pangborn in pale reprises of their more felicitous thirties roles.

As the nominal leads, Paige and DeFore are a particularly disagreeable duo. Jack Carson as Peter Virgil, the hapless private eye, gives a thoroughly professional performance, actually managing to mitigate the seamier implications of his rather unpleasant character.

Although she receives fourth billing, the show belongs to Doris Day. Director Curtiz was an old hand at constructing sympathetic frameworks for the introduction of potential stars (such as Errol Flynn in *Captain Blood* and John Garfield in *Four Daughters*), and this film is no exception. While not exactly a stunning debut for her talents, *Romance on the High Seas* is a perfectly respectable showcase for the introduction of the blonde-haired, blue-eyed singer to the moviegoing public.

Doris Day dominates the film from our first glimpse of her staring in the window of the travel agency. Attractively groomed, her neatly tailored gray suit and hat complementing her fire-engine red blouse and handbag, she looks

ROMANCE ON THE HIGH SEAS (1948). With Jack Carson

rather unprepossessing until she opens her mouth. She's Georgia Garrett, a gum-chewing honky-tonk singer from Far Rockaway who plans elaborate vacations all the time just for the hell of it. As a struggling singer in a dive called the Club Casa, she's hardly in a position to afford such trips, but the sheer thrill of outlining the itinerary simply "fractures" her. (She's had seven passport pictures taken, she informs a travel agent, but never as a blonde.)

Day was an instant hit in *Romance on the High Seas*. She was the prototypical girl-next-door, without the tearful blandness of a June Allyson or the whimpering helplessness of a Jeanne Crain. Viewing this film today, one is immediately struck by her directness. Her jaunty, extroverted demeanor suggests that, while she may not have the dough to take that cruise to South America *this* year, she is fully confident that she'll go some day—and in high style.

And of course she *does* go, sooner than she expected, and gets a husband (Carson) in the bargain. Thus, Day's Georgia Garrett is the self-assured personification of the American ethos that if one thinks positively, works hard, and seizes the opportunity at hand, one's dreams will all come true. If Day's animated exuberance is a bit more persistent than spontaneous in *Romance on the High Seas*, she was still inexperienced, and her performance might not seem so relentlessly energetic if she were not surrounded by such lackluster co-stars as DeFore and Paige.

The split between Day's acting and her singing in the film is marked. While she comes on like a forties hepcat in most of her dialogue scenes (one of her less endearing terms for people she likes is "chootch"), she puts over her several songs with a natural élan rare for a newcomer. The eloquence she lends such relatively mediocre Jule Styne-Sammy Cahn songs as "It's You or No One" and "Put 'Em In a Box" is a welcome relief from the boundless gusto she exudes in her straight acting.

The musical highlight of the film is Day's rendering of "It's Magic," which along with "Secret Love" and "Que Sera Sera," are the three songs she introduced in movies that are most closely identified with her. She sings the song to Carson at a small café in Havana during one of the stopovers on the cruise. The music begins under the dialogue as two guitarists sing the lyric softly in Spanish. When Day begins singing, Curtiz dollies slowly in to her, with one of the guitarists dominating the right foreground of the frame.

Curtiz lets Day sing most of the song in either a closeup or a medi-

ROMANCE ON THE HIGH SEAS (1948). As Georgia Garrett

um shot with Carson. By the end of the number, the guitarist has strolled behind the couple to join her in the very last lines of the song. It is a lovely moment, the high point of the film, in fact. The emotional directness and utter sincerity with which Day's voice and eyes endow "It's Magic" convince the viewer that he is watching some crazy kind of magic itself, specifically the emergence of a star.

Going to the movies was a national pastime in those deceptively complacent years following World War II, and *Romance on the High Seas*, released in June 1948, satisfied most of the undemanding customers for whom sitting in air-conditioned theaters was a pleasant way to escape the heat for a couple of hours. Doris Day more than satisfied the customers, however; *Film Daily* reflected the general consensus when it effusively predicted that "Day is going to be spelled dough at the box office, from here on out."

The prophecy proved accurate. The public took Day to its heart immediately; here was a down-home gal with whom everyone in the audience could identify. Warner Bros. quickly perceived that their lengthy search for a major musical star had ended. Janis Paige's contract was allowed to expire, and June Haver, whom the studio had borrowed from Fox for a couple of pictures, was forgotten while the studio wheels began revolving around Doris Day. The publicity department worked overtime establishing and nurturing her corn-fed image of bright-eyed effervescence and cheerful optimism. She was at once dubbed "The Golden Tonsil" and "The Tomboy With a Voice." Coinciding with the release of her first movie, Day's recording of "It's Magic" became a runaway hit single, and she was also reaching

WARNERS' MUSICAL SWEETHEART

millions of radio listeners as a singer and leading lady on Bob Hope's NBC program. A hit in three media at the age of twenty-four, Doris Day had definitely arrived.

Now that Warner Bros. had their big musical star, however, they really didn't know what to do with her. The musical was not a genre in which this studio excelled. Most of their successful entries in the field had been the Busby Berkeley marathons of the thirties and such elephantine, "fictionalized" biographies of the forties as *Night and Day* and *Rhapsody in Blue*. Warner Bros. movies were famous for their gritty realism and social consciousness; the more gossamer ingredients of the musical had always eluded them.

Neither did the studio have the resources nor personnel to produce a musical of wit and style. Most Warners musicals of the late forties and early fifties seem oblivious to the experiments and extensions of the genre that were occurring simultaneously at MGM. Directors such as Vincente Minnelli and Stanley Donen, and artists like Judy Garland, Fred Astaire, and Gene Kelly were expanding the form in vital, unique directions. Dance, song, narrative, and char-

On Bob Hope's radio show (1948)

acter were being woven together in integrated structures whose possibilities seemed endless.

When one compares the plethora of talented performers, directors, choreographers, designers, and orchestrators who were working at Metro with the unimaginative crew employed in Burbank, it's a miracle that Day survived these early years at all. Time and again, her individuality and professionalism transcended the mediocre direction of David Butler and Roy Del Ruth, the vulgar, overblown musical arrangements of Ray Heindorf, and the unspeakable dance direction of LeRoy Prinz.

The studio *was* shrewd, however, in assigning Day roles that emphasized the similarities between her private self and her public persona. In most of her Warners films, Day is the brash extrovert attempting to crash the big time, undaunted by failure, resilient and indefatigable. There is little room here for either melancholy self-pity or quiet introspection. The only manifestations of self-indulgence Day exhibits are an occasionally voracious appetite and an unlimited enthusiasm for life, love, and professional success, not always necessarily in that order.

My Dream Is Yours (1949) integrates the diverse elements of Doris Day's developing persona into a far more satisfying whole than her de-

but film. Day plays Martha Gibson, an aspiring singer employed by the Metropolitan Music Company, who is "discovered" by agent Jack Carson when she imposes her voice over an instrumental version of "Canadian Capers," plugged into a juke-box conveniently located in her uncle's bar. Carson hopes to pose her as a threat to his former client, popular singer Lee Bowman, who has terminated Carson's services out of vanity and pique.

Carson's dogged efforts to make her a star don't get very far, until he realizes he's been using the wrong approach, changes his tactics, and eventually catapults her to national stardom. In its skeletal outline, the plot resembles a hundred other movies, but scenarists Harry Kurnitz and Dane Lussier have a twist or two up their sleeves. Bowman is an incipient alcoholic, and Day gets her big chance when he has gone on one of his binges, too loaded to go on the air. Matters are complicated further by the fact that Day, who has become romantically entangled with Bowman, is unaware that Carson's enterprising efforts on her behalf have developed from professional motives into personal ones.

In its fascinating mixture of ambition and naïveté, Martha Gibson is characteristic of several roles Doris Day was to play. A widow with a small son, Day momentarily

MY DREAM IS YOURS (1949). With Jack Carson

hesitates when Carson informs her that taking the child to Hollywood might hamper her career. Ambition triumphs over the maternal instinct, however, and after a tearful farewell, Day leaves the boy in New York with her uncle. (Carson later sends for the child to cheer her up when success fails to come immediately.)

This combination of artlessness and aggression permeates Day's personality. Her ingenuousness and ambition co-exist in a most comfortable alliance; both traits seem totally instinctive, so that the overall impression is one of easy charm rather than cold calculation. When her lack of funds forces her to move in with Carson's colleague (Eve Arden), Day's natural ebullience wins over Arden's initial, and understandable, resistance to the imposition. Day really does impose herself, too. In their shared bedroom, Arden finally accepts this invasion of her privacy with wry equanimity, even selling her car to finance Day's career.

Somehow, through all of this,

MY DREAM IS YOURS (1949). With Lee Bowman and Jack Carson

MY DREAM IS YOURS (1949). With Jack Carson

Day manages to convey the excitement of a young girl on her first date. Out for a night on the town with Lee Bowman, she tells him she feels like a "rainbow fizz." She's so distracted by her first audition in Hollywood that she forgets to remove the price tag from her new dress. Her unbridled energy poses certain problems for Carson, however. When he arranges an audition for a potential sponsor of a radio show (S. Z. Sakall), Day performs a wildly animated rendition of an incredible song about geiger counters and atomic energy that would be tasteless if it weren't so terrible. When she finishes, Carson says to Sakall, "Great little personality, hasn't she?" The perpetually befuddled Sakall replies, "Yes, and so much of it."

When Carson hears Day singing a lullaby to her son, he realizes that he has been selling her in the wrong manner. He calms her down, increases the number of warm ballads in her repertoire, and after she substitutes for the drunken Bowman, her success is assured.

My Dream Is Yours was also directed by Michael Curtiz, and his work here is far superior to *Romance on the High Seas*. The opening portions of the film are amusing, with their satirical thrusts at the world of advertising, radio, all-girl orchestras, and matinée idols. Curtiz evokes a darker tone in his delineation of the *A Star Is Born*-like relationship between Day and Bowman. Although not as fully realized as it might have been if the film had tilted more toward drama than comedy, there is still a disturbing edge to the later scenes when Day, now a star, continues to pine after Bowman while Carson waits helplessly in the wings.

In the final scene of the film, Day buttresses Bowman when he falters in the middle of a comeback quietly engineered on his behalf by Carson. She picks up the song where Bowman has paused, and they finish it together as a duet. An added poignancy is achieved by the fact that the song, "My Dream Is Yours," is the same one she had sung on the radio show in which she had replaced Bowman.

Instead of expressing gratitude for helping him save face, Bowman tells her that their impending marriage precludes the possibility of two careers in one family. Naturally he feels he should concentrate on *his* career. Only now does Day see Bowman's true character, and she leaves him for Carson. The ending remains ambivalent however; we are never certain what has motivated her decision—the realization of Bowman's real nature, or the knowledge that Carson would never ask her to sacrifice her career.

Day's acting in *My Dream Is Yours* is far more restrained and

IT'S A GREAT FEELING (1949). With Jack Carson, Bill Goodwin, and Dennis Morgan

varied than in her first film, and she is surrounded with a superior cast as well. Eve Arden once again demonstrates that she's the best friend a star ever had, and Jack Carson gives one of the most affecting performances in a career that was always overlooked and sadly underrated. Only Lee Bowman strikes a sour note as the recalcitrant singer; he's so consistently unsympathetic that one begins to question Day's continuing attraction to him.

Although *My Dream Is Yours* is shot through with music, much of it is thrown away or merely used in the background while the dialogue continues. Since the music is by Harry Warren and the lyrics are by Ralph Blane, however, the snatches of song that punctuate the narrative are insouciant and melodious. Especially lovely is Day's rendering of the standard, "I'll String Along With You," which she sings to her son in an effort to lull him to sleep.

The one big production number is an animated dream sequence in which Day and Carson perform an energetic vaudeville routine with Bugs Bunny. The scene is arbitrarily imposed onto the film, especially since it represents the dream of Day's son, a character whose viewpoint we have not previously shared.

Day was reunited with Carson for her second film in 1949, *It's a Great Feeling*. Their third and last movie together, *It's a Great Feeling* is an uninspired affair, a type of movie peculiar to the forties in which a studio would kid itself by casting its big stars as themselves while ostensibly allowing their avid fans a glimpse behind the scenes. A little of this self-congratulating "satire" goes a long way, particularly when the situations and dialogue are as contrived and humorless as Jack Rose and Mel Shavelson's.

Their scenario takes as its start-ing point the conceit that none of Warners' top directors wants to direct Carson's newest co-starring opus with that tremulous tenor, Dennis Morgan. Producer Bill Goodwin decides to let Carson direct the film himself. When Morgan refuses to act if Carson directs, the latter enlists the aid of Judy Adams (Day), a waitress in the studio commissary.

Posing as Carson's pregnant wife, she fools Morgan into signing the contract out of sympathy for her plight. Once he has Morgan's signature, however, Carson's problems are not over. Every female star on the lot turns down the lead, so the two guys reconcile their differences in an effort to convince Goodwin he should take a chance on the unknown Day.

Day runs the gamut in *It's a Great Feeling*. She impersonates Bette Davis, a grieving wife in widow's weeds, and last as well as least, a French chanteuse with the moniker Yvonne Amour, complete with black wig and Montmartre outfit. Day attacks her role with her customary gusto, but her performance here is even more sanguine than in *Romance on the High Seas*.

Director David Butler lets her mug mercilessly. Every time she confronts the beleaguered Goodwin on the lot, she begins batting her eyelashes and pulling her teeth over her lower lip a la Bugs Bunny,

*IT'S A GREAT FEELING (1949). With Harlan Warde,
Eleanor Parker, and Patricia Neal*

accompanied by strange little tweets on the sound track. This schtick is repeated *ad nauseam*, as Day gamely disguises herself as an elevator girl, waitress, cab driver, and dental assistant in order to get the producer's attention. Finally, when every maneuver has failed, Day heads home to Wisconsin to marry her childhood sweetheart—Errol Flynn.

In addition to Flynn, just about every major star under contract to Warner Bros. makes an appearance in *It's a Great Feeling*. Sydney Greenstreet laughs, Gary Cooper slurps a soda in a drug store and says "Yup," Jane Wyman faints, Ronald Reagan gets a haircut, and Joan Crawford gets hysterical. At the top of the film, directors Raoul Walsh, King Vidor, Michael Curtiz, and David Butler himself play cameos, each one successively declining Goodwin's offer to direct the picture.

Despite the galaxy of stars and personal appearances, *It's a Great Feeling* is not very good. It was the first film in which Day worked under Butler (she was to make five more movies with him), a mediocre contract director who had put Shirley Temple through her paces in *Bright Eyes* and *The Little Colonel*. Day does have one outstanding number in the film. Reflecting on her love for Morgan as she speeds through the night on the train to Wisconsin, Day sings the beautiful Jule Styne-Sammy Cahn ballad, "Blame My Absent-Minded Heart." The song and its singer combine to evoke a mood of inexpressible longing and regret. Day is never more disarming than in this atypical moment of quiet repose.

The year 1950 ushered in the decade of Doris Day. She was voted "the girl we would like to take a slow boat back to the States with" by U.S. servicemen in Korea, won the Laurel Award as "the leading new female personality in the motion picture industry," and starred in three movies, one of which, *Tea for Two*, was one of the top grossers of the year.

In her first film of the year, *Young Man With a Horn*, the singer undertook a role that was a change of pace from the energetic ingenues she had been portraying. Even though she received co-star billing above the title, Day's role is secondary to the tempestuous relationship between Kirk Douglas and Lauren Bacall that dominates the film. Day is so quiet and unobtrusive that one frequently forgets she's even in the movie, and it is very difficult to retain a clear image of her once the film has ended.

Young Man With a Horn's episodic narrative recounts the rise to fame of an orphan-turned-trumpet player who marries a society temptress (Bacall), neglects his old friends, and almost drinks himself to death when his stormy marriage disintegrates. Suggested loosely by the life of jazz musician Bix Beiderbecke, Edmund H. North and Carl Foreman's script is strikingly similar to the one Foreman had penned a year earlier for Douglas, *Champion*, which was also a "poor-boy-makes-good-until-he-meets-a-rich-dame" affair.

THE DECADE OF DORIS DAY

Young Man With a Horn reveals at once the strengths and weaknesses of Michael Curtiz as a director. The film is superficially well made; the early scenes are suffused with the ambience of lonely Southern towns, back street jazz dives, and seaside ballrooms. Curtiz' refusal to adopt a point of view toward the characters or their predicaments, however, deprives the film of real depth or ambiguity, rendering much of the melodrama hollow and diffuse when it should be resonant and precise.

Douglas gives one of his most *angst*-ridden performances as Rick Martin, a man obsessed with hitting that elusive, unattainable high note. It is difficult to take his relationship with Bacall seriously, because the moment he meets her, he has her number as a bored dilettante who ruthlessly plays with people's lives. And yet inexplicably, he falls madly in love with her, marries her, and nearly lets her selfishness destroy his career.

Curtiz injects some fever into their final confrontation when Bacall breaks his beloved records,

*YOUNG MAN WITH A HORN (1950). With Kirk Douglas
and Lauren Bacall*

severs the relationship, and informs him that she's found a "lady friend" who understands her. It's not stated in so many words, but the look Bacall gives this "lady friend" suggests that she has now decided to dabble in Lesbianism.

Day remains on the periphery of the action. As Jo Jordan, a big band singer whose rise to fame parallels Douglas', she drifts in and out of the narrative, turning up only when he needs a boost in ego or a few words of quiet encourage-

ment. Her relationship to Douglas is never made explicit. At one point she tells Hoagy Carmichael that Douglas brings out the mother instinct in her, but at other times she seems more like a pal or a sister. Then again, in the scene when she discovers Douglas has married Bacall, Day behaves like a spurned lover, running from the room in a flurry of tears.

The scenarists obviously view Day as a combination Cassandra-confidante. Early in the film she

38

YOUNG MAN WITH A HORN (1950). With Kirk Douglas

warns Douglas that he's married to his trumpet, and that this obsession will preclude the possibility of viable human relationships. As he packs his suitcase after being fired from the dance band for which she sings, Day advises him that the only item he needs to pack is his horn. She is with him at the end, however, as he battles pneumonia and alcohol in his struggle toward self-awareness.

Jo Jordan herself is a celluloid creation not far removed from the real Doris Day, when she was just the kid with the vocal chords, traveling from town to town on one-night stands. Although the songs in *Young Man With a Horn* are subordinated to the drama, Day's subdued renderings of "With A Song in My Heart," "The Very Thought Of You," and "Too Marvelous for Words" are smooth and mellow, perfectly capturing the style and tone of the big band singer she is playing. For once, even Ray Heindorf's musical score is appropriate, a rich jazz flavor permeating the bluesy, smoky orchestrations.

With her following film in 1950, *Tea for Two*, Doris Day moved into the upper echelons of film stardom. She had top billing for the first time in her career, played opposite Gordon MacRae in the first of a series of box-office successes they made together, and the film itself, incredible as it may seem to-

YOUNG MAN WITH A HORN (1950). With Kirk Douglas and Lauren Bacall

TEA FOR TWO (1950). With Gordon MacRae and S. Z. Sakall

day, was one of the year's biggest hits.

Suggested by the twenties musical comedy, *No, No, Nanette*, filmed twice before in 1930 and 1940, *Tea for Two* emerges as a tired rehash of the same plot Warner Bros. had used for countless musicals since *42nd Street*. It's the one about the talented neophytes putting on a show but unable to raise enough cash to begin rehearsals. MacRae is the composer, Gene Nelson the lead hoofer, and Day plays Nanette, the

stage-struck Long Island heiress who tries to finagle $25,000 out of her uncle (S. Z. Sakall), to invest in the show.

The permutations of the plot are all too familiar to fans who dote on this sort of nonsense. Sakall has been ruined in the stock market crash, but he promises his niece the money on a bet if she will say "no" to every question she is asked for twenty-four hours. Naturally he expects her to relent and say "yes" before the day is over, but Sakall underestimates our spunky hero-

TEA FOR TWO (1950). Dancing with Gene Nelson

ine. With the help of her secretary (Eve Arden), she wins the bet, and finally, after a few more complicated plot maneuvers, the show goes on with Nanette in the lead and becomes a dazzling Broadway success.

Tea for Two could serve as a textbook for what was wrong with most of Warners' musicals. Employing a pointless flashback structure, the film opens with Day and MacRae's children and their teeny-bopper friends cavorting in their parents' old clothes. Uncle "Cuddles," who miraculously is still alive after twenty-one years and hasn't aged a bit, takes the unappreciative youngsters for a stroll down memory lane, and the action recedes to 1929. Anachronisms abound throughout the movie. The clothes and hairstyles in the flashback look more fifties than twenties (Day plays half the film in pedal pushers). No attempt is made to capture the authentic look and feel of the period.

When Day hospitably offers her Long Island mansion as a rehearsal hall, the whole film begins to resemble a third-rate stock version of *Wish You Were Here*, with numbers by the pool, on the lawn, etc.. Never has putting on a show looked like more fun. All the chorus girls ever do is sit around eating sandwiches and diving into the pool.

Very little of Vincent Youmans'

lovely original score for *No, No, Nanette* is used in this bowdlerization. Additional material by Youmans, Al Dubin and Harry Warren, and George and Ira Gershwin replaces the deleted songs, and as delightful to hear as these tunes are, their charm is undercut by LeRoy Prinz's inept staging and Ray Heindorf's cacophonous arrangements.

As the songwriting hero, MacRae is colorless and bland; he never seemed at ease in front of the camera, and sensing this perhaps, the studio wisely saw to it that in all of his films with Day, it is *she* who gets more songs, more closeups, and more footage in general. Gene Nelson is pleasant enough, but his roles in these films were always poorly defined. He seldom had a love interest, and his particular brand of athletic tap-dancing lacked excitement and spontaneity. (The fact that he was always saddled with Prinz's choreography didn't help his career either.)

Eve Arden steals every scene in which she appears; S. Z. Sakall does his usual (he gets himself wound up in ticker tape in this one); and Billy DeWolfe, as the director of the show, is the butt of several tasteless references to his "afflictions" and "difference" from other people. DeWolfe's androgynous persona was usually held up to ridicule in the movies he made, thus obscuring his genuine abilities as a

THE WEST POINT STORY (1950). With Gordon MacRae

clown and farceur.

Even though Doris Day is the star of *Tea for Two*, she is not as omnipresent as one would expect. Her performance is actually rather good, considering the material and David Butler's tepid direction. Her playing had become more consistent, and her level of energy was more controlled and assured. Although her dancing in the film leaves much to be desired, she sings the variety of songs given her with considerable aplomb. Her phrasing of the title song, specifically the tenderness with which she infuses the words "sugar cake," reveals the progress she has made since *Ro-*

mance on the High Seas. With each successive film, Day was perfecting and refining her prodigious resources which would develop into the unabashed joy and self-assurance she would exude in her greatest musical films.

Day's last film in 1950, *The West Point Story*, hardly qualifies as one of the latter. Gordon MacRae and Gene Nelson are again putting on a show, but this time it's the annual "100th Night" production at West Point. Designed primarily as a vehicle for James Cagney, who plays a down-at-the-heels director sent by MacRae's producer-uncle to entice the boy to Broadway, *The West*

STORM WARNING (1951). With Steve Cochran and Ginger Rogers

LULLABY OF BROADWAY (1951). With Gene Nelson

Point Story represents the Warner Bros. musical at its nadir.

Day plays Jan Wilson, a movie star whom Cagney had discovered years ago when he took her out of the chorus. As a favor to her mentor, who has been forced to become a cadet, she treks to West Point to be MacRae's date for the Saturday hop, winds up falling in love with him, and agrees to stay at the academy and participate in the show in order to be near him.

In 1951 Doris Day made four movies; won her first *Photoplay* Gold Medal Award (for *On Moonlight Bay*); and married Martin Melcher on her twenty-seventh birthday. Melcher was an amiable ex-song plugger who became Day's agent, molding and altering her image at will, judiciously choosing her parts until his death in 1968. More than anyone else, it was Melcher's shrewd judgment of the public pulse which sustained his wife's popularity and recharged her career during the seventeen years that followed.

Storm Warning, Day's first venture that year, provided the actress with her first serious dramatic role. It was also the first, and last, film in which she played a character who dies. (As the pregnant wife of Steve Cochran, Day is shot to death by the Ku Klux Klan.)

Daniel Fuchs and Richard Brooks' screenplay bears a marked similarity to *A Streetcar Named Desire*. Ginger Rogers plays Day's older sister, a somewhat overripe neurotic who comes to visit, is intimidated by her burly brother-in-law (Cochran), and becomes romantically involved with trial prosecutor Ronald Reagan. The Ku Klux Klan forms a swirling background for this melodrama directed by Stuart Heisler.

Neither Day's fans nor the critics were too impressed with her initial foray into straight drama, and the actress soon returned to the standard fare that was expected of her. Her next movie, *Lullaby of Broadway*, is yet another potpourri of old songs, sentimental romance, and show business clichés concocted by house director David Butler. As a chorine looking for her derelict mother, Day breezes through the film with her customary bounce and verve, singing a brace of standard songs, but despite her efforts, she is unable to conceal the fact that *Lullaby of Broadway* is a blatant attempt to duplicate the box-office success of *Tea for Two*.

Gordon MacRae is mercifully absent, but Gene Nelson brings a new dimension to the word "bland" as Day's co-star. Also on hand are the ubiquitous S. Z. Sakall and the indefatigable Billy DeWolfe. As Day's boozer of a mother, Gladys George milks the role for the little it's worth (and then some), contributing the one bright spot to the film with her rendition of "In a Shanty in Old Shantytown."

Day's third film that year, *On Moonlight Bay*, is one of the movies for which she is most fondly remembered. Extremely successful at the time of its release, it confirmed Day's popularity with moviegoers. She won the *Photoplay* Gold Medal Award for her role in the film, an award bestowed at that time by the readers of *Photoplay* magazine who would cast their votes annually for their favorite male and female star performances.

Viewed today, one's immediate impression of *On Moonlight Bay* is its marked inferiority to the masterpiece it so obviously wishes to emulate, Vincente Minnelli's *Meet Me in St. Louis*. The slides over the credits, with the last one springing to life; the casting of Leon Ames as the father; the structure determined by seasonal changes; and even Day's auburn wig, all invite comparison with the earlier, better film.

Adapted from Booth Tarkington's "Penrod" stories, Jack Rose and Melville Shavelson's scenario begins with the Winfield family moving into a new neighborhood

ON MOONLIGHT BAY (1951).
Marjorie Winfield at bat

and ends a year later with Day marrying the boy next door, Gordon MacRae. During the intervening time, we are treated to the shenanigans of Day's younger brother (Billy Gray), Leon Ames' growing awareness of his own mortaiity, and Day's emergence from a ball-playing tomboy into a radiant young woman in love.

Roy Del Ruth's direction is yeomanlike, but he never captures the special magic of that bygone era immediately preceding this country's entry into World War I. The actions of the characters are quaint and forced. At no time do they reflect a different era and morality. Del Ruth is content to emphasize the "cuteness" of a situation rather than discover the common truth at its core. For instance, MacRae spouts radical slogans when he is in college, even ripping up a five-dollar bill on Ames' front porch (of course, Day's father is a banker). Then later, after his stint in the service has "matured" him, MacRae recalls his radical days as a mere folly of callow youth. This kind of smarmy pandering to middle-class complacency pervades the film. By constantly sentimentalizing its characters and their problems, Del Ruth detaches us from any real concern or emotional involvement.

On Moonlight Bay might easily be dismissed as an inconsequential piece of candy-coated nonsense if it were not for Doris Day. Her Marjorie Winfield is a formative role in the development of a persona that was increasing in popularity with every picture. She's a *bona fide* tomboy in pigtails when we first glimpse her carrying an armchair through the front door. She's willing to help her mother (Rosemary De Camp) with household chores, but she prefers playing baseball with the neighborhood team. When she makes it to third base on her first hit, she is instantly accepted as "one of the boys."

Boys as romantic objects don't interest her much, until she meets her new neighbor (MacRae), a senior at the University of Indiana, who has "wild" ideas about marriage being slavery for a woman and prison for a man. She doesn't attempt to change overnight for him, however; even though she enlists the aid of two powder puffs to boost her natural endowments on their first date together, she still munches popcorn as he tries to woo her in a rowboat on Moonlight Bay. Later in the film, when a rival suitor serenades her, she obliviously devours an apple. Day's love life never interfered with her appetite.

Gradually, however, Day forsakes the baseball diamond for dancing lessons. She sprouts bangs, ties ribbons in her hair, and replaces her plaid pinafores with soft

ON MOONLIGHT BAY (1951). With Gordon MacRae

feminine dresses of pale blue, yellow, and green. Her transformation seems certain when MacRae first kisses her; her free hand discreetly knocks her cap and baseball to the floor.

This passage from carefree tomboy to boy-crazy young girl connected with female adolescents in the audience. Day may have been the girl next door, but even the girl next door eventually had to grow up, leave home, and get married. There is a kernel of truth in the romanticized puberty rites Day undergoes in *On Moonlight Bay*. The very fact that she suffered through this transitional period in a girl's life separates her immediately from the sex goddesses with whom she was contemporaneous.

Day's last movie in 1951 was another all-star fiasco, *Starlift*, in which she and other Warner Bros. stars entertained the troops in San Francisco waiting to be airlifted to Korea, as well as the wounded returning from the front. When Day bursts into a base hospital to cheer the boys, one soldier asks the blonde star to prove she's really Doris Day to his buddy on the telephone. Day picks up the receiver and breaks into a rousing chorus of "Lullaby of Broadway."

The star made two films in 1952, the first of which, *I'll See You In My Dreams*, is a musical biography of lyricist Gus Kahn. *I'll See You In My Dreams* is something of a revelation, a bio-pic that never insults the intelligence and is often quite affecting. Not the least surprising element of the film is Danny Thomas' muted performance as Gus Kahn. The unctuousness that Thomas has exuded on television for years is totally absent in his playing here; it is certainly his finest hour in any medium.

Michael Curtiz' low-key direction details Kahn's early years, his platonic working relationship with Grace LeBoy (Day) who writes the music for his first hit song, their eventual marriage, his Broadway success and collaboration with composer Walter Donaldson (Frank Lovejoy), and his declining years in Hollywood. All the accoutrements of the conventional biography are present, but there is an intensity and passion in the playing between Thomas and Day that makes one care about their lives, their failures as well as their successes.

Day is excellent in the film. Her playing has never been warmer or more controlled. (Her appetite remains unchecked, however; when Thomas offers to share a salami on pumpernickel with her at the top of the film, she devours the whole sandwich while he watches helplessly.) She takes the initiative in their relationship, her inner strength providing the necessary

STARLIFT (1951). With Ruth Roman

I'LL SEE YOU IN MY DREAMS (1952). With Danny Thomas

balance for his more erratic behavior. Eventually, Thomas becomes so dependent on her that he leaves her temporarily. He resents the fact that she treats him more as a child than a husband, never letting him make any professional decisions.

Instead of the "and-then-he-wrote" type of numbers that characterize most films of this sort, Curtiz effectively parallels each song with a stage in the couple's relationship. When Thomas composes "Pretty Baby" at an after-hours jam session, the exhausted Day falls asleep in a chair at one of the tables in the night club. Softly finishing the song so as not to awaken her, Thomas descends the platform, picks her up in his arms, and gently carries her out of the lounge, their receding figures gaining a poetic dimension in a long shot as the music diminuendos. The ambience of the jam session, with its smoky atmosphere, evocative lighting, and waiters stacking chairs onto tables is beautifully captured, and Curtiz heightens the sequence by filming it in one continuous take.

Equally lovely is the scene that occurs on the morning following the birth of their second child. Thomas has been out all night, composing the lyric for "It Had to Be You," and when he appears shamefacedly in Day's hospital room, he presents her with the song before she can question his whereabouts. Day begins to recite the verse slowly, as Walter Donaldson's haunting melody begins on the sound track.

As she reads the words that convey the depth of his love for her, Thomas takes the lyric from her and sings the chorus in a quiet, faltering voice. It is a superb moment, masterful in its simplicity and taste. What could have been unbearably maudlin becomes extremely touching in the exchange of glances between Thomas and Day.

Day herself does full justice to all of her solos. She helps a movie audience follow the bouncing ball while she leads them in "Gee, I Wish I Had a Girl"; she wins over an obstinate group of backers and producers with her heartfelt audition of "The One I Love Belongs to Somebody Else"; and her interpretation of the title song has the simple directness of the greatest popular singing.

Curtiz' eloquent direction of *I'll See You In My Dreams* transcends the limitations of a genre that has produced few good movies, with the notable exception of *Yankee Doodle Dandy*, also directed by Curtiz.

Day's second venture in 1952 was another biographical movie, *The Winning Team*, indifferently directed by Lewis Seiler. This filmization of baseball immortal Grov-

I'LL SEE YOU IN MY DREAMS (1952). As Grace Kahn

THE WINNING TEAM (1952). With Ronald Reagan

er Cleveland Alexander's life traces his rise through the bush leagues to become a dynamo pitcher for the Philadelphia Phillies and the Chicago Cubs. Hit on the head by a baseball in 1911, he begins to experience double vision, repeatedly passes out on the field, and is eventually forced into involuntary retirement. The movie ends when he returns to the mound in a blaze of glory by winning the 1926 World Series for the St. Louis Cardinals.

Seiler's direction of this testament to endurance and resilience is flat and diffident, but then confronted with Ronald Reagan as the beleaguered pitcher, who can blame him? It's Reagan's show all the way, and he carries it exactly nowhere.

As his nagging but loyal wife, Day has little to do but stand around and look concerned. *The Winning Team* was the actress' second straight drama, and it would be her last until *The Man Who Knew Too Much* in 1956. While the movie did no measurable damage to Day's career, *The Winning Team* more or less finished Reagan in motion pictures, a distinction one can view with mixed gratitude, depending upon one's political persuasions.

By the end of 1952, Doris Day was earning $2500 a week at Warner Bros. and was the star of her own CBS radio program. She also had a minor skirmish with the studio when she adamantly refused to reteam with Danny Thomas in a remake of *The Jazz Singer*. (Peggy Lee eventually played the role.)

All three of the star's 1953 releases were directed by David Butler. The first, *April in Paris*, is an innocuous musical in which the singer's brash exuberance collides with Ray Bolger's sly, attenuated dancing style. Butler had directed the film version of Bolger's Broadway success, *Where's Charley?*, a year earlier, and the studio assumed that casting the rubber-legged dancer opposite their star singer would ring bells for everyone concerned.

Day plays Dynamite Jackson, a Broadway chorus girl who has never been to one place she can't reach by subway. When a bumbling bureaucrat in the State Department (Bolger) erroneously mails her Ethel Barrymore's invitation to represent the American theater at the International Festival of the Arts in Paris, the stage is set for a series of mistaken identities and romantic complications.

Mistaking Bolger's error for an inspired act of egalitarian chauvinism, his superiors endorse Dynamite Day as their representative, and they sail together for France. Predictably, Day and Bolger fall in love, are married aboard ship by a busboy caught pilfering liquor in

APRIL IN PARIS (1953). With Claude Dauphin and Ray Bolger

the captain's cabin, and then set about consummating their illegal marriage amidst a series of coy plot contrivances.

When Bolger procrastinates about informing his fiancée (Eve Miller) that he has married Day, the star is confronted with a plot device that was to recur in many of her films. Often, the males who become enamored of Day are not as direct and honest with her as she is with them. Successful songwriter Robert Cummings poses as a garage mechanic in *Lucky Me*, hardened newspaperman Clark Gable pretends to be a journalism student in *Teacher's Pet*, and the endless masquerades Rock Hudson assumes to seduce her are typical of the kinds of deception men are willing to practice on the unsuspecting Day.

Ironically, Day's forthright attitude in her relationships with men renders her superior to the masculine duplicity with which she repeatedly must cope. In the films that share this characteristic of the male as imposter-aggressor, it is Day, the ingenuous innocent, who is finally more sympathetic and worthier of our concern. Thus, in *April in Paris*, Bolger's dilatory nature seriously undercuts our involvement with his character. He's not really good enough to wind up with Day. We know it, and she knows it too.

Dynamite Jackson is a real Doris Day heroine. The affinities to Gerogia Garrett in *Romance on the High Seas* are obvious. Both are struggling singers, both yearn to travel, and both get their wish through similar quirks of fate. Once aboard the ship, Day's extroverted behavior proves too much for the staid delegates accompanying her to the Paris festival. She drops an olive at dinner, chews celery loudly, and uses her dessert spoon for the bouillon. Preferring steak and potatoes to a New England boiled dinner and poached eggs, she excuses herself for lowering the tone of this "pallbearers' convention" and proceeds to dance with a waiter.

April in Paris boasts an enchanting score by Vernon Duke, with lyrics by E. Y. Harburg and Sammy Cahn. Day's delicate phrasing of the title song imbues its lyric with a melancholy that is most affecting. The film's musical highlight, "I'm Gonna Ring the Bell Tonight," is a rollicking dance performed by Day and Bolger in the kitchen of the ocean liner. Even LeRoy Prinz seems to have been inspired by Duke's music; it may well be the best number he ever staged.

In an effort to duplicate the success of *On Moonlight Bay*, Warner Bros. mined Booth Tarkington still further and came up with Day's sec-

APRIL IN PARIS (1953). With Ray Bolger

ond 1953 offering, *By the Light of the Silvery Moon*, in which we are back with Marjorie Winfield and her family. Day has regressed to tomboy behavior while MacRae has been away fighting World War I. When first seen in the film, she's underneath a jalopy doing some repair work. When she emerges, there's a smudge or two on her rosy cheeks, but the auburn hair of the earlier film is now peroxide blonde, an indication perhaps of the authority and control which are by-products of superstardom.

When MacRae returns home, he wants to postpone their marriage until he's doing well enough at her father's bank to support them. When she insists on going to work also so that they can marry sooner, he will have none of it. Her readiness to take a job proves that Day's practicality has remained intact. (During the war emergency, she has even been working around Ike

Hickey's garage to earn some extra money.) She is clearly the one with both feet on the ground in this relationship. When MacRae's jalopy breaks down on one of their dates, Day jumps out of the car and repairs the jammed gas valve (he doesn't even know where the gas tank is).

If *By the Light of the Silvery Moon* has the edge on its predecessor, it is primarily due to David Butler's relative superiority to Roy Del Ruth as a director, and to Donald Saddler's inventive staging of the musical numbers. A bit of housecleaning among Day, MacRae, and maid Mary Wickes is transformed into an impromptu jig during "Ain't We Got Fun?". The couple's duets, "Your Eyes Have Told Me So" and "If You Were the Only Girl," have a surplus of warmth and feeling. Even MacRae loosens up considerably in the exhilaratingly staged "Just One

Girl." (This was the singer's fifth, and last, film with Day.)

The big production number, "Chanticleer," is somewhat over-produced for the intimate musical to which *Silvery Moon* aspires, but it is distinguished by some unusually athletic dancing and lusty vocalizing by Day. The star struts barefoot through the number, dressed in the quintessential Doris Day costume of this period in her career—lavender overalls with a pastel patch on one leg and a red handkerchief hanging out of the back pocket, a saffron blouse, and little red ribbons tied onto her blonde pigtails.

Doris Day next appeared in the best movie she made during her seven years under contract to Warner Bros. *Calamity Jane* (1953) has its prototype in Irving Berlin's masterpiece *Annie Get Your Gun*, but the former has it all over its MGM counterpart with Betty Hutton.

Everything works in *Calamity Jane*. For once, Day has a leading man, Howard Keel, who can hold his own in their scenes together. The music by Sammy Fain and lyrics by Paul Francis Webster are rich and varied, giving Day her quota of ripe comedy numbers such as "Deadwood Stage" and "Just Blew In From the Windy City," as well as the lovely ballad "Secret Love" that was to dominate the hit parade long after the movie had disappeared from theaters.

BY THE LIGHT OF THE SILVERY MOON (1953).
With Mary Wickes

BY THE LIGHT OF THE SILVERY MOON (1953).
With Gordon MacRae

Even David Butler mysteriously rises to the occasion, helped immeasurably by Jack Donohue's sprightly direction of the musical numbers. Butler and Donohue effortlessly integrate the songs into James O'Hanlon's screenplay, lending the movie a rhythmic flow characteristic of the best film musicals. Butler stylizes the Western setting just enough, capturing the proper tone and framework for his characters to burst into song and dance.

O'Hanlon's original screenplay depicts Calamity Jane's simultaneous efforts to bring live entertainment to the stage of Deadwood City and grab a husband for herself. Traveling to Chicago to convince singer Adelaide Adams (Gale Robbins) to return with her out West, Day mistakenly engages Robbins' stage-struck maid (Allyn McLerie) for the journey.

McLerie soon becomes the toast of Deadwood City, and the two girls, who have become fast friends, renovate a log cabin and move in together as roommates. Their friendship evaporates, however, when Day learns that the army officer she's had her eye on (Phil Carey) is in love with McLerie. Day's anger subsides once she realizes that her continual sparring partner, Wild Bill Hickok (Keel), is the man for her, and the finale finds everyone reconciled and dedicated to living happily ever after.

Doris Day is terrific as Calamity Jane. At last she has a role she can sink her teeth into, and she takes it by the reins and races through the film at a gallop. Outfitted in buckskin from head to toe, with a Confederate cap on her dirty blonde hair, a red kerchief around her neck, six-guns around her waist, boots on her feet, and little make-up on her face, Calamity Jane is Day's definitive characterization during the first epoch of her stardom.

The tomboy aspect of Day's persona receives full expression here, but her swaggering bravado conceals a feminine vulnerability essential for audience sympathy. Day is never masculine or abrasive; she brings dimension to the role by capturing the contradictions in Calamity's character, her brusque, independent nature as well as that softer side of her which yearns ultimately for emotional commitment to a man.

Qualities that have been implicit in many of Day's previous characterizations surface in *Calamity Jane*. Her behavior has never been more aggressive. She pursues Phil Carey dauntlessly, rescuing him from a pack of Indians, glamorizing herself to attract him, and on discovering that her best girl friend has won his heart, shooting a glass of punch out of McLerie's hand. Her aggressive behavior manifests itself in more positive ways as well, when her concern for the lonely men of Deadwood City and the future prosperity of the town motivates her trip to Chicago to enlist the services of Adelaide Adams.

Day's encounters with Keel are particularly lively. He sees through her sham and tall tales. When she

CALAMITY JANE (1953). In the title role

CALAMITY JANE (1953). With Dick Wesson and Paul Harvey

embellishes the number of Indians she held off during a stagecoach attack and exaggerates the death count involved in her rescue of Carey, Keel asks her why she never fixes up her hair. The easy familiarity of their animosity belies their affection for one another, however, and it comes as no surprise when they belatedly discover that each has been chasing the wrong person.

When Day sings "Secret Love," she seems transformed—not just through her love for Keel, but, more profoundly, through the attainment of self-awareness. Whenever she has tried to be a "lady" before, vestiges of the tomboy always

remained. When she wore a beautiful yellow dress to visit a sick neighbor, she went barefoot and fell in the creek on the way home. Similarly, when she attended the Fort Scully annual ball, she wore Custer's old army coat over her soft pink gown.

Now as she triumphantly carols her love for Keel, she is paradoxically more feminine than ever, even dressed in riding shirt and jodhphurs. The spaciousness of the setting—the open country with its trees, green grass, clear brook, and blue sky—conveys the feeling of release that has prompted her exultant outburst. Day's singing of "Se-

CALAMITY JANE (1953). With Howard Keel

cret Love" achieves the rarefied stratosphere of the greatest musical numbers—it literally takes off and soars.

Jack Donohue's contribution to *Calamity Jane* landed him the directorial chores on Doris Day's subsequent vehicle, *Lucky Me* (1954). Released with much ballyhoo as Warner Bros.' first musical in CinemaScope, *Lucky Me* tries hard to be spontaneous and original but succeeds only in looking forced and tired.

Day plays Candy Williams, a singer with a troupe called the Parisian Pretties. (The other members of this unlikely little band are Phil Silvers, Nancy Walker, and Eddie Foy, Jr.) Stranded in Miami after being kicked out of a burlesque house, the group pays off a meal they enjoyed in an expensive restaurant by working in the kitchen for a few days.

Songwriter Robert Cummings is ensconced in the hotel adjacent to the restaurant, working on a score which he hopes the father of his fiancée (Martha Hyer) will like well enough to bankroll for Broadway. Although Day levels with him on their first meeting that she's momentarily working as a dishwasher, Cummings poses as a garage mechanic in order to make time with her. It's only a matter of time and a few well-placed musical numbers before Day sings his songs better than he could have imagined in his wildest dreams, and charms Hyer's father (Bill Goodwin) into backing the show with Day herself in the lead and big fat parts written in for her three cronies.

Doris Day is the sole point of interest in *Lucky Me*. Characteristically cheerful and buoyant, her unflagging optimism is joined in this instance to a superstitious nature which borders on the obsessive. Seeing thirteen people in the audience, she leaves the stage. While walking down the street, she avoids black cats, stepping on cracks, and walking under ladders.

Lucky Me had bad luck itself at the box-office. (Surprisingly, *Calamity Jane* had shown a similar drop in profits from other Day musicals.) The musical movie was slowly being eroded as a viable genre. Costs were becoming prohibitive, the foreign market for such entertainment was dwindling, and television specials and revue hours were offering people for free what they had been paying money to see in theaters.

Sensing this development, Marty Melcher suggested to his wife that she incorporate herself, while he negotiated the termination of her contract with Warner Bros. Day was reputed to have a yearly income of $500,000 in 1954. In addition to her movies, she was recording an average of twelve singles a year, whose annual sales approached the five million mark.

LUCKY ME (1954). As Candy

LUCKY ME (1954) With Robert Cummings

For her last film under contract to her home studio, Melcher chose a property which he released through Warner Bros. under the auspices of his independent company, Arwin Productions. *Young at Heart* (1954) was intended to bridge the gap between the carefree musicals in which Day had been starring and the more demanding, challenging roles Melcher envisioned for her future.

In this quasi-musical remake of Michael Curtiz' *Four Daughters* (1938), Frank Sinatra, in the role that brought John Garfield stardom, plays Barney Sloan, a self-pitying piano player who is hired by Day's composer-fiancé (Gig Young) to orchestrate his songs for a forthcoming Broadway show. When Day realizes that one of her sisters (Elizabeth Fraser) is hopelessly in love with Young, she leaves him standing at the altar and elopes with Sinatra.

After a year of estrangement from her beloved family, she and Sinatra return home for Christmas. His mysterious despair has increased after a year of marriage, however. Borrowing his brother-in-law's car during a raging snowstorm, Sinatra cuts off the windshield wipers, lets the ice freeze over, and presses his foot down on the accelerator. Day then gets to repeat the speech she made to Kirk

Douglas in *Young Man With a Horn*. Visiting Sinatra in his hospital room, she refuses to allow him the privilege of quitting. When her entreaties get no results, she tells him she is pregnant. Suddenly he has a change of heart, survives surgery, and in no time at all, everyone is gathered around the piano again, laughing and singing.

Young at Heart is a peculiar hybrid of a film. All of the scenes involving Day and her musically inclined family collide with the darker aspects revolving around Sinatra. Part of the problem lies in scenarists' Julius J. Epstein and Lenore Coffee's failure to pinpoint the specific nature of Sinatra's malaise; he appears to be merely an uninteresting loser who loves to wallow in his own misery. An added drawback is director Gordon Douglas' inability to integrate the disparate elements of the narrative into a cohesive whole.

Even more damaging is the total lack of rapport between Day and Sinatra. They each seem to be acting in a different film. The script gives them no real love scenes together. They talk a great deal about how much they mean to each other, but they never touch, never kiss, never embrace. There is no passion or commitment between these two characters, and combined with the thinly veiled animosity Day and

YOUNG AT HEART (1954). With Frank Sinatra

YOUNG AT HEART (1954). With Gig Young, Frank Ferguson, Frank Sinatra, and Elizabeth Fraser

Sinatra generate toward one another as actors, the net effect is more than a little unpleasant.

Young at Heart really has little to recommend it. Many of the scenes where the family gathers around the piano for an evening musicale are unintentionally humorous. Father Robert Keith plays the flute, daughter Elizabeth Fraser plays the violin, Dorothy Malone the harp, and Day doubles as singer and pianist while the reas-

suring figure of aunt Ethel Barrymore knits in the background.

The original score by James Van Heusen and Mack Gordon is pedestrian, with the striking exception of the hauntingly beautiful "You, My Love." All of Sinatra's solos, however, are standards, and he has never sounded better on such classics as "Someone to Watch Over Me," "One For My Baby," and "Just One of Those Things."

From 1955 to 1957, Doris Day starred in the three movies in which she gives the best performances of her career. In *Love Me or Leave Me*, *The Man Who Knew Too Much*, and *Pajama Game*, Day successfully submerges and integrates her persona into the character she is playing so that our response to her is conditioned not by her personality, but by the nature of the role itself.

Day's first appearance in a film after terminating her contract with Warner Bros. was in an MGM musical. *Love Me or Leave Me* had originally been planned for Ava Gardner, but when the cameras finally rolled, it was Doris Day who was portraying Ruth Etting, the twenties chanteuse whose tempestuous relationship with a small-time Chicago thug inspired Daniel Fuchs and Isobel Lennart's screenplay.

Love Me or Leave Me is no ordinary musical biography. It opens with Day as a "dime-a-dance" hostess in a Chicago speakeasy. Manhandled by one of her customers, she loses her job and is taken under the wing of Marty Snyder (James Cagney), a hood who strongarms the illegal clubs into using his laundry service. Cagney's pull in the underworld, and her genuine talent as a singer, insure her rise to fame in Chicago, but once they branch out into radio and Broadway, his jealousy begins to hamper her career.

CHALLENGES AND EXTENSIONS

After a disastrous scene backstage on her opening night in the Ziegfeld Follies, Day helplessly agrees to marry Cagney. They tour nightclubs all over the country until Hollywood beckons with a movie contract. Once on the West Coast, Day is reunited with Cameron Mitchell, a pianist who had come between her and Cagney in Chicago. Now a leading conductor at the studio where she is working, Mitchell resumes his courtship of Day. Insanely jealous, Cagney shoots Mitchell in front of his house and goes to prison. Feeling she owes Cagney a great deal after all he has done for her, Day pays his bail and headlines the nightclub he has renovated in Hollywood, as the film ends.

Although *Love Me or Leave Me* is dominated by James Cagney's mercurial performance as the crippled gangster who is slave to an obsession he cannot articulate, Doris Day matches him every step of the way. Her Ruth Etting is a radical departure from any of her previous roles. From the moment we see her in the dance hall, chewing gum and shaking her body to the music as she waits behind the rope for a customer, this is definitely a Doris Day with a difference.

Day simultaneously captures

LOVE ME OR LEAVE ME (1955). As Ruth Etting

LOVE ME OR LEAVE ME (1955). With James Cagney

Ruth Etting's tough exterior and her inner vulnerability. Ruthlessly ambitious, she is literally ready to claw her way to the top until Cagney's convenient appearance in her life offers her a comfortable short cut to success.

Day never lets us forget that success and fame are uppermost in Etting's mind. When she admits to Mitchell early in the film that her ambition doesn't leave much room for anything else, she isn't kidding. Eventually she becomes Cagney's mistress, and finally marries him when his hold on her has proven so pervasive that she can no longer function without him.

LOVE ME OR LEAVE ME (1955). As Ruth Etting

LOVE ME OR LEAVE ME (1955). With Cameron Mitchell

The sexual tension in the twisted relationship between Cagney and Day is the real dramatic meat of *Love Me or Leave Me*. Many of their frenzied quarrels contain sado-masochistic overtones which are truly disturbing. When the action shifts to Hollywood, and Day renews her affair with Mitchell, a slackening of the tension occurs, and the film suffers accordingly.

Apart from the stellar performances of its two leads, *Love Me or Leave Me* is a movie of bits and pieces. Director Charles Vidor lacks a strong visual style, and his use of CinemaScope is quite awkward, leaving vast areas of the

*THE MAN WHO KNEW TOO MUCH (1956). With Bernard Miles,
Brenda de Banzie, and James Stewart.*

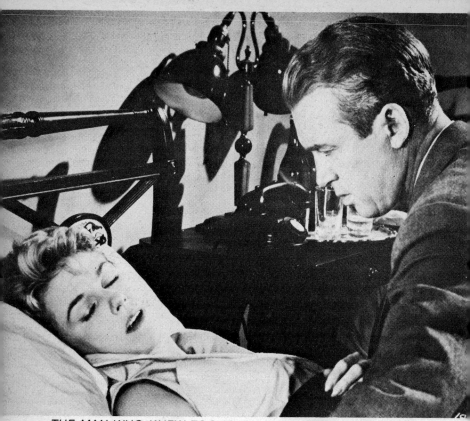

THE MAN WHO KNEW TOO MUCH (1956). With James Stewart

screen empty for uncomfortably long periods of time. Although Vidor effectively captures the twenties milieu during the first half of the film, the later scenes in Hollywood are sterile and anachronistic.

Vidor's direction of the musical numbers also leaves a great deal to be desired. He allows few closeups of Day while she is singing, and during several numbers that are integral to the development of the narrative, he inexplicably keeps the singer in extreme long shot. Specifically, the emotional power of the ending is undercut by the fact that we only see Day singing the title song in long shot. Vidor saves the closeups for Cagney, who is watching her at the bar.

The one "all-stops-out" production number, "Shaking the Blues Away," is clumsily staged. Vidor has better luck with the more

THE MAN WHO KNEW TOO MUCH (1956). With James Stewart

intimate songs, particularly "Ten Cents a Dance." Day sings this Rodgers and Hart classic in a tight black dress with sequins. She has never looked sexier, and her appreciation of her body, her awareness of her sexuality, is exhilarating. When she plants her feet squarely on the floor with arms akimbo, one has only to look into her eyes as she sings, "Come on, big boy, ten cents a dance" to know that the girl next door has long since learned the facts of life.

Day sings many of the songs associated with Ruth Etting in *Love Me or Leave Me*, including "You Made Me Love You," "It All Depends On You," and "Mean To Me." Two new songs were written for the film: "Never Look Back" by Chilton Price, and "I'll Never Stop Loving You" by Nicholas Brodszky and Sammy Cahn.

THE MAN WHO KNEW TOO MUCH (1956). As Jo McKenna

(Day's recording of the latter made the "Top 100" chart for popular records, which *Billboard* began publishing in 1955.)

It is a tribute to Day's abilities as a singer and an actress that her Ruth Etting captures the essence of that archetypal heroine of the twenties, fragile yet courageous, vulnerable yet indisputably single-minded in her desire to reach the peak of her profession.

Day's fans responded affirmatively to her different image. The fact that she played one scene in her petticoat and hit the booze rather heavily in the later portions of the film actually seemed to increase her popularity. *Love Me or Leave Me* turned out to be one of the biggest grossers of 1955. The star certainly profited from its success, because in addition to her $150,000 salary for the film, she was guaranteed 10 percent of the gross after the initial costs had been recouped. The success of the film induced Metro to sign Day to a contract for five films for the total sum of $900,000.

Day's next movie, *The Man Who Knew Too Much*, presented her with the most challenging part of her career, and the actress responded with a performance of nerve-shattering intensity. The film was Day's first opportunity to work under a director of the caliber of Alfred Hitchcock, and, unfortunately, it would also be her last.

Hitchcock is a master at revealing aspects of his actors' personae that have remained untapped in their previous screen incarnations. His handling of such diverse personalities as James Stewart, Cary Grant, Ingrid Bergman, and Grace Kelly at once undercuts and amplifies their mythic proportions.

Similarly, the director penetrates Doris Day's sanguine image, simultaneously exposing the neurotic underpinnings and extending its larger implications. Hitchcock explores Doris Day—the actress, the singer, the personality—with a scrutiny that mercilessly lays bare her weaknesses as well as her strengths, her limitations as well as her potentialities.

In the film Day and her physician-husband (James Stewart) are vacationing in Morocco with their small son when they witness the murder of an acquaintance they have made. The victim's dying words to Stewart reveal that a political assassination will occur shortly in London.

Before Stewart can disclose this information to the Moroccan authorities, however, he learns that his son has been kidnapped by the unassuming English couple (Brenda de Banzie and Bernard Miles) that he and Day had befriended the previous evening in a restaurant. The distraught parents fly to London, and, alternately helped and hindered by the police, ultimately rescue

JULIE (1956). In the title role

their child after a series of stunning Hitchcockian set pieces in a taxidermist's shop, a secluded chapel, a concert hall, and the foreign embassy of the assassination target.

Released in the summer of 1956, *The Man Who Knew Too Much* is vastly superior to the version which Hitchcock filmed in England in 1934. The remake gains through its expressive, psychological use of color, the formal demands of the VistaVision process in which it was filmed, and especially in the extra care the director takes to probe the relationship between the husband and wife.

Hitchcock's portrayal of man's limited perceptions is illustrated in the opening shot of the film. We immediately view a typical American family (Stewart's) sitting in the back of a bus. As the camera tracks backward, the strangeness of their surroundings is revealed; the other passengers are mostly Arabs. From this moment, nothing is as it seems in the film. Hitchcock moves from the apparent harmony of that initial image through a series of increasingly unbalanced compositions, culminating in the regained harmony of the final reunion between mother, father, and child.

The implication of shared guilt which runs throughout Hitchcock's films receives full expression in *The Man Who Knew Too Much*. Frantic at learning that the foreign official will be assassinated at a con-cert in Albert Hall, Day flees to the hall, where she is confronted with a terrifying moral dilemma. The ominous figure who knocked at their hotel room in Morocco approaches her in the lobby and warns her that her son's safety is contingent on her silence during the concert.

In one of the most extraordinary uses of montage in films, a sequence running twelve minutes without dialogue and composed of one hundred twenty-four separate shots, Hitchcock conveys Day's dawning realization that this man is going to assassinate the prime minister who is sitting in the opposite box. Our concern is engaged on an immediate level by *our* knowledge that the shots will be fired when the cymbals clash during the cantata. On a deeper moral level, however, we are concerned for Day, who is torn between fear for her son's life and fear for the life of a total stranger.

Hitchcock's extension of time during this sequence is brilliant. The duration of each shot increases the suspense as the music builds to its climax. We watch helplessly in pity and awe as Day sobs hysterically, clinging to the red drapes for support, the fate of two human lives thrust upon her conscience.

The scream that rips from her throat as the assassin fires is consistent with Hitchcock's Catholic

PAJAMA GAME (1957). With John Raitt and Carol Haney

view of the world, which absolves the sacrifice of one's own son if another human life is at stake. Paradoxically, her scream saves not only the prime minister's life, but also precipitates the trip to the embassy which will end in the recovery of her child.

Day's emoting during this sequence is remarkable. It is arguably the finest acting she has ever done, but there is another, earlier scene in *The Man Who Knew Too Much* which approximates its power. When Stewart learns that their son has been kidnapped, he procrastinates telling his wife until they have returned to the hotel. Opening his medicine bag, Stewart selects two sedatives and forces her

to wash them down.

Hitchcock's choice of angle, lighting, and crosscutting between the couple heightens the audience's anticipation of her reaction. As she gets groggier and starts to lie down on the bed, Stewart finally tells her. Rising from the bed, she pounds him with her fists, cursing him for giving her sedatives, and threatening to kill him before she collapses in his arms. Day's hysterical response is harrowing to watch, but the actress handles this difficult scene with superb control.

Maternal obsession is a recurring theme in Hitchcock's movies, and the intimations on motherhood that are woven into *The Man Who Knew Too Much* simultaneously illuminate certain facets of Day's screen image and the character she is playing. Before Day married Stewart, she had been a successful musical comedy star on Broadway. His unwillingness to practice medicine in New York required her premature retirement from the stage.

There is every indication in the narrative that their life in Indiana is not as rosy as it could be. In the opening scenes of the film they quarrel incessantly, contradicting one another over the most trivial matters. She makes veiled references to her aborted career, and he seems to resent the rapport between her and their son. (Ironically, the denouement of the film forces Stewart to utilize his wife's talent in a life-or-death issue. It is her singing of the nursery song, "Que Sera, Sera," and their son's reply by whistling the tune from his hiding place in the embassy, which enables Stewart to rescue the child.)

Her excessive attachment to her son has replaced the career she relinquished to marry Stewart. She has apparently directed all of her emotional energy into the boy in a subconscious effort to punish her husband. When she and Stewart are walking in the Moroccan marketplace, she even asks him when they can have *another* child. If, as Molly Haskell has suggested, this maternal devotion verges on a neurotic form of overcompensation, Hitchcock ruthlessly undercuts the depth and validity of Day's feelings toward her son following the murder in the marketplace. As Day stands paralyzed by shock and fear, it is Brenda de Banzie, the "kind" English lady, who spirits the child away from the gruesome scene.

Therefore, before we are thirty minutes into the film, we see that Day is inordinately possessive toward her child, yet at the same time incapable of shielding him from the most horrible act he has ever witnessed. When we discover later that she has recently been over-dependent on pills, a composite picture emerges of a woman on the brink of an emotional breakdown. Her hysteria in the scene where she learns of her son's abduction is cathartic. Not only does it release the tension that has been accumulating within *her*, but it also exorcises the fear and concern *we* have felt for her survival.

Inexplicably dismissed by critics at the time as inferior to the original, *The Man Who Knew Too Much* is indisputably one of the central works of Alfred Hitchcock's career. Furthermore, Doris Day's Jo McKenna is the perfect antidote to the "superannuated virgin" image of her that has persisted into the seventies. The performance remains her supreme triumph during the twenty years she reigned a star.

The song by Jay Livingston and Ray Evans which Doris Day intro-

PAJAMA GAME (1957). Singing "I'm Not at All in Love".
At her right: Barbara Nichols

duced in *The Man Who Knew Too Much*, "Que Sera, Sera" (Whatever Will Be, Will Be), was among the top best-selling records for twenty-seven weeks in 1956. Since its initial release, the song has become more or less identified with Doris Day, and its cheerful stoicism supposedly parallels the actress' own personal philosophy. She *must* like the song, because she has since reprised it in *Please Don't Eat the Daisies* (1960) and *The Glass Bottom Boat* (1966). It was also the theme song for her television program.

The singer had two other record hits on *Billboard*'s weekly chart in 1956, "The Party's Over" (which appeared for eleven weeks) and "Julie" (ten weeks). The latter was the title song to Day's subsequent film, a "damsel-in-distress" item written and directed by Andrew L.

Stone. Stone and his editor-wife turned out a series of small-budget films in the fifties, all of which were photographed in their entirety on actual locations. Thus *Julie* actually occurs all over the Monterey Coast as Day is chased from Carmel to San Francisco, and eventually up into the air, by her murderous husband Louis Jourdan.

Day begins screaming the moment the credits end, and she seldom stops during the course of the movie. Its wildly improbable climax finds stewardess Day landing an airplane after a multiple shootout in the cockpit.

After the nonsensical melodramatics of *Julie*, the actress returned to musicals to play the lead in *Pajama Game* (1957). The original Broadway cast of the long-running musical hit was transferred *in toto* for the film version, with the exception of Barbara Nichols as Poopsie and Day as Babe Williams. (It is one of the unending ironies of Hollywood casting that Janis Paige, who had the nominal lead in Day's first movie, *Romance on the High Seas*, originated the role of Babe on Broadway.)

Pajama Game also marked Day's return to Warner Bros. for the first time since 1954. She was obviously chosen for the role by co-directors George Abbott and Stanley Donen to counterbalance the negligible box-office draw of such Broadway names as John Raitt, Carol Haney, and Eddie Foy, Jr.. As commercially inclined as the choice might have been, it resulted in one of the happier casting coups of the decade. Doris Day gives one of the definitive musical comedy performances in *Pajama Game*.

Pajama Game is not only the best adaptation of a hit stage musical for the screen; it is also one of the classic film musicals. It is difficult to determine who was responsible for what in the tandem direction, but the joy and vitality that burst from every frame in the film are reminiscent of Donen's best work.

The best musical movies all share a consistency of style and more precisely, an assurance and certainty of style that pervade the entire film. Donen is a master at discovering the proper style a musical requires; viz. *On the Town, Singin' in the Rain,* and *Funny Face*. It is in this delicate tightrope-walking between the fantasy world of the musical and the everyday world of "realistic" cinema that Donen's greatest achievement lies. This achievement approaches the sublime in *Pajama Game*, where the workaday world of the Sleep-Tite Pajama Factory is magically transformed into a stylized musical comedy. Disputes between labor and management become the matter of softshoe routines and hillbilly love songs. A company picnic explodes into one of the most exciting dance numbers in films, as Carol Haney and friends joyously celebrate their "Once-A-Year Day." Color, decor, gesture, and movement are carefully coordinated throughout the film, but nowhere more happily than in this picnic sequence. The green grass, sparkling lake, multi-colored pennants, and Haney's orange-and-gold petticoats, combined with the sheer physicality of Bob Fosse's choreography, communicate a euphoric abandon that is irresistible.

The screenplay that Abbott and Richard Bissell adapted from their book of the stage play (which in turn was based on Bissell's novel, *7 1/2 Cents*) is remarkably true in tone and spirit to its Broadway source. Although three numbers from the original were cut for the

PAJAMA GAME (1957).
With John Raitt

film version, each of the songs omitted—"A New Town Is a Blue Town," "Her Is," and "Think of the Time I Save"—served more as scene-changers on the stage than as vital links to either story or character. Donen's decision to eliminate Haney's "Jealousy Ballet" is also consistent with his inclination to forego the dream ballets that were becoming predictable necessities in most film musicals of the fifties.

Pajama Game's numerous songs and dances revolve around the romantic and professional conflicts between a new superintendent (Raitt) and the impetuous head of the union's grievance committee (Day) in the Sleep-Tite Pajama Factory, located in a small midwestern town. Various subplots involving time-study man Foy's irrational jealousy of Raitt's secretary (Haney), management's juggling of the books, and the determined efforts of labor to get a 7 1/2-cent raise, fill out the narrative. What makes *Pajama Game* unusual is the fact that it is one of the few musicals to deal with the people of the working class, whose work is an integral part of the plot. Totally unsentimental, Abbott and Bissell's book has a tough, hard-boiled edge to it that never wavers.

Doris Day's Babe Williams is every bit as tough and hard-boiled as her surroundings. From her first entrance, striding in to confront Raitt with a complaint from an abused worker, Day takes command of the screen and never relinquishes it. Munching half-eaten apples, defying a drunken Foy to knife the apple on top of her head at the picnic, or jamming a machine when Raitt halts a workers' slowdown, this is a brassy, no-nonsense dame.

Day's vulnerability as an actress, however, gives the character that necessary extra dimension. Her love scenes with Raitt, especially the "Small Talk" sequence with its lyrical backdrop of rain softly falling outside as the couple spar, tease, and finally make love, are genuinely affecting. Her repeated protestations to Raitt about how much the union means to her are earnest and sincere. The entire performance is totally believable. The persona of Doris Day and the character of Babe Williams merge until the distinction between actress and role becomes inseparable.

Day beautifully integrates her characterization into her musical numbers in *Pajama Game*. Seldom had she been given such a terrific score to sing, and she makes the most of it. (The promise of *Pajama Game*'s composer-lyricists, Richard Adler and Jerry Ross, was cut short by Ross' tragic death after their second hit, *Damn Yankees* opened on Broadway in 1955.)

Day's first number in the film, "I'm Not at All in Love," is in-

PAJAMA GAME (1957). The finale, with the entire cast in pajamas

vigorating. She commands and defines the space within the frame by her expressive use of physical gesture. When she points, the viewer's eye instinctively follows the gesture. Donen builds the song to a rousing climax in which Day resolutely shakes her head and stomps her feet, reasserting that "she's not at all in love," as the camera pulls back, the music soars, and Donen dissolves to the annual picnic banner being hung up over the entrance to the factory.

Day is alternately tender and sexy in the "Small Talk" number with Raitt. The expression on her face when she lights a match to cook him an omelet is highly erotic. With the lit match poised in her hand and her face turned expectantly toward his, he embraces her waist and blows out the match. The sensuousness of this scene contrasts sharply with the ebullient high spirits of the number that immediately follows, "There Once Was a Man." This raucous, raunchy love duet is perhaps the musical highpoint in the film for both Day and Raitt.

Day's intuitive way with a melody, her ability to phrase a song in order to draw the maximum impact from its lyric, is evident once again in her reprise of "Hey There." Evocatively set against the changing colors of the railroad crossing signal lights outside her window, Day begins the song in a romantic reverie. She sings to herself in the mirror, moves to the foot of the bed, and rouses herself to a more realistic appraisal of her situation with the words, "Get on the ball, girl," pounding the brass footboard of the bed with her fist, clearing her head with a restless shiver.

On the words, "You used to have such pride," she moves to the side of the bed and lies down, the red neon from the signal light outside illuminating both the room and her face. The number ends as she loses control of the lyric, weeping softly on the bed. Day's performance of this song is a superb example of acting *through* song, and is only one of the moments that constitute some of the most memorable acting of her career.

Despite its excellence, *Pajama Game* was not a financial success. 1957 was a transition year for the musical. In addition to *Pajama Game*, such heavyweight entries in the genre as Stanley Donen's *Funny Face*, George Cukor's *Les Girls*, Rouben Mamoulian's *Silk Stockings*, and George Sidney's *Pal Joey* were released. Only *Les Girls* and *Pal Joey* did above-average business at the box office. With each subsequent year, fewer musicals were produced until by the mid-sixties, the only manifestations of this most joyous form of filmmaking were such inflated dinosaurs as *The Sound of Music* or *Hello, Dolly!*.

With the decline of the genre in which she had excelled for nearly ten years, Doris Day's popularity began to wane slightly. Although she had proven her thespic abilities in *Love Me or Leave Me* and *The Man Who Knew Too Much*, it was becoming obvious to Martin Melcher that his wife's image would have to undergo some kind of metamorphosis if she intended to stay on top. Most of the dramatic roles offered her were redolent with the new permissiveness in sex and language that was infiltrating Hollywood movies in the late fifties, and the actress adamantly refused to play any part which she thought might annoy her fans or tarnish her image.

If 1957 was the transition year

VAMPING TILL READY

for the musical, then 1958 was a transition year for its golden-voiced exponent. The two films in which she starred in that year lay the groundwork for Doris Day's third era of stardom, a period during which she would attain greater popularity and success than ever.

Day's first movie in 1958, *Teacher's Pet*, contains in embryonic form the basis for her subsequent comedies with Rock Hudson. Continuing a pattern established by her relationships with Ray Bolger in *April in Paris* and Robert Cummings in *Lucky Me*, Day is a straightforward heroine who is deceived by the sexually aggressive male (Clark Gable).

When Day, an unlikely instructor of journalism at a night college, invites the city editor of the *New York Evening Chronicle* (Gable) to speak to her class, he retorts with a condescending letter which states in hard-boiled terms that the only way to learn about the fourth estate is through experience. Ordered by his publisher to apologize to Day for the brusque tone of his letter, Gable visits the class.

Infatuated with the sexy blonde instructor, Gable enrolls as a student. Telling her that he's in the

TEACHER'S PET (1958). With Clark Gable

wallpaper business, Gable astounds Day with the excellence of his classwork. Gable gradually woos Day away from his rival, a stuffy psychologist (Gig Young), but eventually she discovers his true identity. Matters are complicated further when Gable expresses his distaste for the Hoosier homilies that characterize the venerated writings of Day's late father, a Pulitzer Prize winner who ran a country newspaper called the *Eureka Bulletin*.

Fay and Michael Kanin's original scenario lets both Day and Gable modify their views in time for the final clinch. He concedes that "experience is the jockey, but education is the horse," and she admits that everything about journalism can't be learned from a textbook.

The Kanins' script, which received an Academy Award nomination for the best original screenplay of 1958, contains many astute observations on the world that revolves around the city desk, and infuses the relationship between the two stars with wry perception and gentle humor. George Seaton's leaden direction continually undercuts script and stars, however. Seaton has one of the dullest visual styles in films, and much of *Teacher's Pet* has an austerity more appropriate to a heavy drama than a romantic comedy.

Once the viewer accepts the disparity in age between Gable and Day, both stars give relaxed and charming performances. Day is amazingly restrained; she had never really played an intellectual before, so perhaps she felt that it would be in character to curb the more gregarious aspects of her personality.

The director's lack of expertise is nowhere more apparent than in his handling of the scenes involving Gig Young. Young, who inexplicably won an Oscar nomination as best supporting actor of the year, mugs outrageously during an interminably belabored hangover scene.

Audiences loved *Teacher's Pet*, though, and it raked in the highest grosses of any Day film since *Love Me or Leave Me*. Her recording of the title song stayed on the charts for twelve weeks, and was joined in mid-summer by "Everybody Loves A Lover," one of the singer's biggest disc successes. A front

runner on *Billboard*'s "Top 100" for fourteen weeks, this song is associated with Doris Day almost as inevitably as "Que Sera, Sera."

Melcher's decision to produce the adaptation of Joseph Fields and Peter De Vries' one-joke stage farce, *Tunnel of Love*, as a vehicle for his wife resulted in one of the star's weakest films. Released toward the end of 1958, *Tunnel of Love* typifies those fifties comedies which subjected the protagonist to endless guilt pangs for a folly he never had the pleasure of enjoying. Richard Widmark spends most of the movie attempting to conceal from his wife (Day) a baby he thinks he conceived with Gia Scala. There is something cruel and in-

TEACHER'S PET (1958). With Gig Young and Clark Gable

sidious in Widmark's suffering, and the bad taste inherent in the material is compounded by the "humorous" references to his wife's inability to bear children.

The leering tone of *Tunnel of Love* was quickly forgotten, however, in the wake of Doris Day's next film. In *It Happened to Jane* (1959), Day is a widow with two children who runs a mail-order lobster business out of her hometown, Cape Anne, Maine. When one of her lobster shipments perishes because of a delay in delivery, Day sues the Eastern & Portland Railroad for the considerable losses and damages.

Dissatisfied with the amount of money the corporation settles on her, the spunky young widow enlists the aid of her lawyer (Jack Lemmon), serves a writ of attachment on Old 97 (one of the E & P's prize coaches), and reactivates her business through the resulting media publicity. Her single-minded attempts to bring the corporation to its knees are checked temporarily when a disgruntled citizenry convince her that she's been placing her own interests above those of the town. However, Lemmon, who is also a Democratic candidate for the first selectman of Cape Anne, rallies the townspeople to support

TUNNEL OF LOVE (1958). With Richard Widmark

IT HAPPENED TO JANE (1959). With Jack Lemmon

her cause, and with their help and encouragement, Day and Lemmon load her lobsters onto Old 97 and take them to market.

It Happened to Jane is a delightful movie, completely unassuming and consistently engaging. Director Richard Quine (*Operation Mad Ball, Bell, Book and Candle*) infuses the narrative with just the right mixture of bucolic whimsy and behavioral charm. The gentle humor of the film is endemic to the rural setting, and Quine effectively integrates the droll situations with the New England eccentricities the assorted characters display. His expressive use of the Maine locales is fresh and invigorating; one can sense the crisp air, the leaves being crunched underfoot, and the aroma

of lobsters resting in the bay.

The personalities of Day and Lemmon are well matched. Especially charming is one of their early encounters when their easy familiarity with one another reveals that they are childhood friends as well as potential lovers. Alternately tender and joking, Day replenishes Lemmon's coffee cup while he outlines his legal tactics for her suit against the railroad. Their reminiscences about Day's late husband and their shared childhood in Cape Anne are intermingled with veiled references to their own developing relationship in an understated love scene tinged with melancholy and humor. The harmony of their playing makes one regret that *It Happened to Jane* remained their

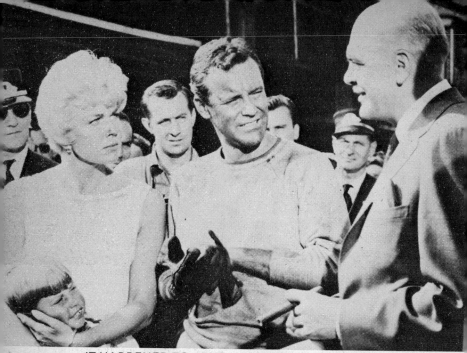

IT HAPPENED TO JANE (1959). With Teddy Rooney, Jack Lemmon and Ernie Kovacs

only film together.

Day's role as *That Jane from Maine*, one of the several working titles for the film, is one of her most characteristic. Playing a widow for the first time since *My Dream is Yours*, Day's ingenuity and self-determination stand her in good stead for her uphill fight against the railroad barons. Dependent on her lobster business for survival, she tackles her battle against the conglomerate with admirable resolve. Each succeeding setback merely intensifies her determined efforts to receive due compensation.

Constitutionally incapable of self-pity, Day's free will and independent spirit are a joy to behold. Faced with a fight before the entire appellate structure of Maine, she removes her shoes on the lawn in front of the court house because her feet hurt and walks barefoot to the car. Her self-assurance wavers only when she thinks her personal battle is jeopardizing the prosperity of the town and the interests of its citizens.

Day's reluctance to consign herself to the role of "languishing flower" characterizes her relation-

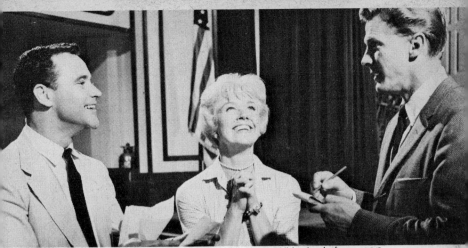

IT HAPPENED TO JANE (1959). With Jack Lemmon and Steve Forrest

ship with Lemmon. Impatient and annoyed because he refuses to propose to her, she goads an offer of marriage out of him as he is stoking coal into Old 97 during the climactic race to market. As Day climbs onto the top of the train in her immaculate white dress, the two yell back and forth at one another in what must be one of the noisiest proposal scenes in movies.

As Day's nemesis, the railroad magnate who opposes her battle for individual rights until the bitter end, Ernie Kovacs is superb. In a sly homage to *Citizen Kane*, Kovacs is made up to resemble the balding Charles Foster Kane in the later scenes of Orson Welles'

masterpiece. Quine implements Kovacs' idiosyncratic performance by subtly designing the various offices out of which he rules his empire in the style of railroad cars.

Eventually however, Kovacs' ruthless megalomania must succumb to Day's indomitability. When Old 97 heads out for market, Kovacs initially routes the train through every whistle stop in New England, hoping the lobsters will spoil before Day and Lemmon reach their destination. By the end of the trip, Kovacs is predictably helping Lemmon shovel coal for more steam, proving that all the power in the world is useless when confronted with Doris Day.

The fortuitous convergence of Marty Melcher, producer Ross Hunter, and writer Stanley Shapiro in 1959 resulted in the film that would make Doris Day the number one female star in the movies—and keep her there well into the mid-sixties. The girl-next-door image was an anachronism by the late fifties, so it was decided to turn the liabilities of that image into a devious kind of asset. Thus, in *Pillow Talk* and the countless mutations that it spawned, Day's moral rectitude is the source for most of the questionable humor.

Basically, all of these comedies pose the same question: How long will it take before Rock Hudson gets her into bed? He finally does get her there, of course, but her honor remains unimpaired because they are married by the time they hit the sheets. Films such as *Pillow Talk* and its indistinguishable off-shoots are responsible for falsely nurturing Day's image as a perennial virgin. She even has an explicit line of dialogue in *Pillow Talk*, where she admits to herself that she's been with a lot of men in her time, but Rock is the jackpot.

What was at stake in these films was not the loss of Day's virginity, but the loss of her integrity as an adult woman. It is this aspect of these interchangeable films that has lasted. Without the stabilizing influence of Day's persona, they would have long since been relegated to obscurity.

Pillow Talk establishes the format that reappears with slight variations throughout most of the remaining films in her career. Interior decorator Day shares a party line with a playboy-songwriter (Hudson). Unable to use her telephone because Hudson is usually setting up his amorous assignations, Day becomes increasingly frustrated and hostile. When Hudson meets her accidentally in a nightclub, he introduces himself as Rex Stetson, an ingenuous ranch-hand who would rather pass on his mother's recipes than make passes at girls.

At first Day is completely taken by Hudson's ingenuousness. For once she feels she has met a man whose mind isn't always on sex. After several dates, however, she begins to wonder if his shyness and good manners aren't hiding some deeper secret, specifically homosexuality. Naturally it's all a carefully constructed scheme on Hudson's part to break down her defenses, get her away to Connecticut for a secluded weekend, and with her resistance lowered by champagne and firelight, finally show his hand.

PILLOW TALK (1959). With Nick Adams and Rock Hudson

There is something intrinsically distasteful in the basic premise behind *Pillow Talk*. Her aspersions on his manhood and his continual references to her frigidity have pathological overtones which remain unexplored by scenarists Maurice Richlin and Stanley Shapiro and director Michael Gordon. The humor is at once coy and prurient. The double entendres that pervade the film are neither funny nor clever. Day advises client Lee Patrick that a fertility goddess is not the item for her Scarsdale home. Patrick's oversexed son, Nick Adams, relentlessly puts the make on Day, easily twenty years his senior. Hudson seduces the female telephone inspector who visits him in answer to Day's complaints. There's even a running joke about Hudson's having a baby.

Accompanying the stag-room humor is a concomitant disdain for the institution of marriage, endorsed only as a means of winding up the plot. In one unfortunate metaphor, Hudson likens the man who gets married to a tree in the forest. Once he goes through the mill, i.e., gets married, he becomes the paper that lines the wastebasket, the vanity table, baby's highchair, etc.. And yet *Pillow Talk* was hailed at the time of its release as a throwback to the classic screwball comedies of the thirties and forties!

It is not difficult to understand why *Pillow Talk* was such a phenomenal success at the box-office. Its mass-oriented components include two larger-than-life stars, beautiful Jean Louis gowns, glamorous cinematography by

PILLOW TALK (1959). With Thelma Ritter

PILLOW TALK (1959). With Rock Hudson

Arthur E. Arling (for the first time, the filters over Day's closeups are visible), and romantic locations in New York City. The movie is painless; it smirks and leers over sex without ever doing anything about it.

Although Doris Day was nominated for an Academy Award for best actress of the year, *Pillow Talk* is not one of her better performances. She overreacts to everything, indulging in three takes when one would suffice. The scene near the end of the film, in which she comes to look at Hudson's apartment before decorating it, is played far too broadly by both stars. As she discovers each successive accoutrement of an apartment designed primarily for seduction—at

the flick of a switch, the door locks, a phonograph goes on, the lights dim, and a bed emerges—the actress indicates her appalled reactions by rolling her eyes up into her head. Her slow burns are far too slow, and her performance generally lacks the control and timing one associates with the greatest comediennes.

Director Gordon doesn't help much either. His idea of a clever use of CinemaScope is to split the screen for Day and Hudson's telephone conversations. One particularly blatant example of sexual innuendo finds both stars taking a bath as they whisper sweet nothings into their respective receivers. As they each put a leg upon the dividing line of the wide screen,

PLEASE DON'T EAT THE DAISIES (1960).
Singing the title song

Hudson starts to move his foot up and down, at which point Day jerks *hers* away. Just in case this inspired bit of business eludes the viewer, Gordon cuts to a closeup of the point where their legs meet.

The casual charm and grace of Day's next film, *Please Don't Eat the Daisies*, are a welcome relief from the one-joke puerilities of *Pillow Talk*. Loosely based on Jean Kerr's anecdotal bestseller, *Please Don't Eat the Daisies* casts Day in the role of Kate Mackay, the pert wife of a Columbia drama professor (David Niven) who has just become the first-string theater critic for a major New York newspaper, and the harried mother of four rambunctious boys.

The rambling structure of Isobel Lennart's screenplay incorporates the family's move from their cramped Manhattan apartment to a house in the country, Niven's platonic relationship with a sexy musical comedy queen (Janis Paige in a lively performance), and Day's efforts to involve herself in the school and community at the expense of her marriage.

When one strips away the considerable glitter of its surface, *Please Don't Eat the Daisies* is basically a television situation comedy in MetroColor and Cinema-Scope. Yet director Charles Walters gives the proceedings a style and sophistication that partially camouflage the flimsiness of the material. The first half of the film is more successful than the second. When Day, Niven, and their brood migrate to the country, it is evident that Walters does not feel as sympathetic toward this milieu as he does toward the more luxurious New York ambience.

Day is utterly charming in *Please Don't Eat the Daisies*. Her relaxed playing of comedy under Walters is totally lacking in the broad strokes which characterize her performance in *Pillow Talk*. Particularly ingratiating is her rapport with the children during the chaos of the opening sequence. Walters' restless camera movements effectively convey the cluttered space of the apartment as Day rushes to dress for a date with her husband. Baby Adam drops water bags out the window, dog Hobo romps around the room in uncontrolled abandon, not one of her boys wants to give Day a goodbye kiss, and when one of them tries to zip up her dress, her flesh accompanies the zipper on its upward flight.

Day and Niven play extremely well together. Walters allows them several lovely long takes in which their genuine feeling and affection for one another unfolds spontaneously, conveying a real sense of two people who, despite all their problems, really *do* belong together.

In *Please Don't Eat the Daisies* Doris Day again embodies an inde-

PLEASE DON'T EAT THE DAISIES (1960).
With Spring Byington and David Niven

pendent, free-spirited woman. She attempts to discover her identity apart from her husband and his profession. When Niven becomes a minor celebrity as a result of his new job, the endless cocktail parties and social obligations that ensue bore Day to distraction. Resenting her peripheral role in his new life style, Day persuades the reluctant Niven that a move to the country will bring the family closer together.

Once there, however, the marriage begins to suffer. Niven spends an increasing amount of time in the city, and Day herself, when she's not repairing the house or painting its rooms, volunteers to work with the local drama club.

Her insistence on contributing in some small way to this drama club is heatedly resented by Niven, especially when he learns that the play they are rehearsing is one of his own, earlier unsuccessful stabs at playwriting. He clearly fails to comprehend Day's need to commit herself to some activity that is separate from his career.

If the pre-women's lib rumblings that periodically surface in the film are necessarily circumscribed by the generic requirements of the material, they *are* there, nevertheless. And when Day transports her family to the country, the move presages the sixties films, such as *The Thrill of It All* and *Send Me No Flowers*, in which the star de-

PLEASE DON'T EAT THE DAISIES (1960). With David Niven

175

MIDNIGHT LACE (1960). With Rex Harrison

serts the city and an exciting career for the plastic environment which would irrevocably congeal her image of headstrong independence.

Please Don't Eat the Daisies was released at Easter of 1960, and its popularity consolidated Doris Day's position as the nation's top box-office attraction. It has been estimated that her profit participation in her movies around this time brought the star approximately one million dollars per film.

For her second outing in 1960, Day unwisely returned to the damsel-in-distress genre. *Midnight Lace* is more sumptuously produced than *Julie*, but it's just as ludicrous and twice as dreary.

As Rex Harrison's American bride, Day finds herself ensconced in a London flat, the victim of pursuits through fog-drenched parks, freak accidents involving stalled lifts and city buses, and anonymous telephone calls which threaten her life.

Any moviegoer past the age of ten should be able to guess the identity of the culprit long before the dénouement, but that doesn't stop director David Miller from planting enough red herrings to keep Day screaming for almost two hours. The actress gives possibly the worst performance of her career in *Midnight Lace*. She plays the entire film on one note of unrelieved hysteria. She whines and screeches, clutches her stomach to express anguish, and in her big breakdown scene, crawls downstairs, clawing at the banisters and steps while emitting strange birdlike noises.

The passiveness of Day's character in *Midnight Lace* is alien to her persona. It is difficult to accept her as a specimen of helpless femininity, a fact that becomes patently clear during the climax of the film when she chooses to risk the precarious girders of a construction site rather than face certain death in her own apartment.

A reteaming of Rock Hudson and Doris Day was inevitable after the success of *Pillow Talk*, so in 1961, shooting began on *Lover Come Back*. This time Stanley Shapiro himself shared co-producing credit with Martin Melcher. The resulting film, released in time for the Christmas holidays, is easily the best of the Shapiro trilogy.

Although the basic plot is the same—Hudson thinks she's undersexed, Day claims he's oversexed—co-scenarists Shapiro and Paul Henning play some reasonably witty and imaginative variations on this one note. This time Day is an account executive for an advertising agency in New York. Fed up with the devious methods her rival Hudson employs to land accounts for his competing agency, Day brings him before the Advertising Council. Hudson persuades showgirl Edie Adams to give false

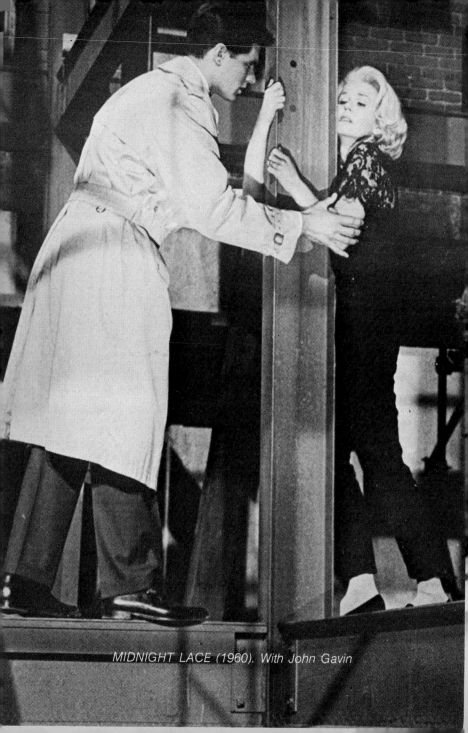

MIDNIGHT LACE (1960). With John Gavin

LOVER COME BACK (1961). With Edie Adams

testimony in his behalf by promising to launch her as the "Vip" girl in a massive new campaign he is planning.

Hudson films several commercials for the non-existent "Vip" to placate Adams, and then shelves them. When Tony Randall, the neurotic vice-president of Hudson's firm, heeds his psychiatrist's advice to assert himself, his first decisive act is the launching of the "Vip" operation.

Thus, an elaborate saturation campaign floods the nation, and Hudson and Randall are confronted with the task of coming up with a product. They enlist the services of Jack Kruschen, a Nobel Prize-winning chemist; but when Day comes snooping around the scientist's laboratory, hoping to land the account herself, she mistakes Hudson for Kruschen. Realizing she doesn't recognize him, Hudson makes no attempt to correct her error. Day wines and dines him, sets him up in a hotel suite, and buys him a new wardrobe, all at her company's expense.

As in *Pillow Talk*, Hudson assumes the role of a wolf in sheep's

LOVER COME BACK (1961). With Rock Hudson

clothing. Pretending to be shy, naive, and sexually inexperienced, he turns Day into the aggressor. She decides to help this "mass of neurotic doubts" prove to himself that he's a man. Just as she's pouring the champagne and laying out her negligée, however, her boss telephones with the information that she has been softening up her nemesis rather than the actual inventor of "Vip."

Kruschen's invention turns out to be a candy-colored mint which enters the bloodstream as pure alcohol; each one is the equivalent of a triple martini. After sampling a few at the Advertising Council, Day and Hudson wake up in a Maryland motel with a certificate of marriage in their possession. Day annuls the marriage, but nine months later, she remarries Hudson as she's being wheeled into the delivery room, convinced that he's reformed his ways and really loves her.

Director Delbert Mann moves *Lover Come Back* along brightly enough, even though he doesn't begin to realize the comic potential implicit in the idea that both Day and Hudson are competing to sell a product that doesn't even exist. Mann also coaxes more felicitous performances out of his two stars than they gave in their previous movie. Hudson, in particular, displays a wry sense of humor toward the proceedings, eliminating the gratuitous movements and gestures which marred his performance in *Pillow Talk*. The maxim that less is more seems to have been lost on his co-star, however. Although her broad playing is somewhat curbed in *Lover Come Back*, Day still doesn't seem to know when she has communicated the comic point of a scene. For instance, her quadruple takes at a strip show are inexcusably overdone.

The actress' role in *Lover Come Back* is in the tradition of the independent women she was portraying around this period. As in *Pillow Talk*, she has a good job with a great deal of responsibility. Brisk and efficient, she relishes her work and attacks her accounts with enthusiasm. She admits to Hudson at one point that she loves the creative challenge of advertising. She is one of the few sixties heroines in movies who has to work for a living, and moreover, enjoys every minute of it.

Furthermore, Day's decision not to sleep with Hudson is not prompted by her virginity (a subject that is never once mentioned in the film), but by her disgust at the elaborate impersonation he has concocted merely to seduce her. Paradoxically, by maintaining her own integrity, she salvages *his* as

LOVER COME BACK (1961). With Rock Hudson

well, paving the way for their eventual reunion in the maternity ward.

If *Lover Come Back* is the relative peak of the Shapiro comedies, *That Touch of Mink* (1962) is easily the nadir. Cary Grant stands in for Rock Hudson on this go-round and Gig Young is the surrogate for Tony Randall, but neither of these capable farceurs can conceal the paucity of comic invention nor the overabundance of leering "humor."

While none of the Shapiro comedies could be called naturalistic, *That Touch of Mink* occurs in a particularly fanciful never-neverland. Seeing Doris Day on the unemployment line within the first five minutes of the film is convincing proof that this movie is operating on a level of reality that defies description. Similarly, the apartment Day shares with Audrey Meadows (who works in the Automat) is lavish enough to raise serious doubts about the morality of these two "working girls."

Day plays an unemployed computer operator who gets swept off her feet by wealthy, romantic business tycoon Cary Grant. Accepting his proposition for a trip to Bermuda against her better judgment, she breaks out in a nervous rash when the crucial moment arises. Determined to sacrifice "everything" for Grant, however, she makes a second stab at consummating their relationship by fortifying herself with liquor. This time, however, Grant discovers her passed out on the hotel bed, the empty bottle stuck onto her big toe.

Finally admitting to herself that she wants marriage to Grant and nothing less, Day arouses his jealousy by going off to Asbury Park with the seedy clerk from the unemployment bureau (John Astin) who has been after her for months. Grant follows her, saving her from a fate worse than death, and on their wedding night, it is *he* who breaks out in a rash.

What all of Shapiro's comedies lack is true wit and style. His characters never develop or change; they are continually subordinated to the plot contrivances, which, by the time of *That Touch of Mink*, have become flaccid with overuse. Delbert Mann's unimaginative direction is unable to erase the bored look from Grant's face, and indulges Day's tendency to mug. (During moments of comic frustration the actress cocks her head to one side and crosses her eyes.) The clarity of Russell Metty's cinematography is considerably lessened by the filters used to arrest both stars' advancing ages.

That Touch of Mink is the one movie that can support the myth of Doris Day as a forty-year-old virgin. There is something fundamentally distasteful in the manner Day zealously guards her innocence in this film, while at the same time encouraging Grant to pursue

THAT TOUCH OF MINK (1962). With Audrey Meadows

her, agreeing to go to Bermuda with him, and then refusing to have sex with him. Day's role in *That Touch of Mink* stands in direct contrast to most of the characters she has played. She is indecisive and circuitous in her dealings with Grant. Her roundabout behavior is totally out of keeping with the straightforward brashness that has characterized her previous relationships with men.

The sour aftertaste of *That Touch of Mink* was eliminated later in 1962, however, when Doris Day starred in *Billy Rose's Jumbo*. Metro had owned the rights to Rodgers and Hart's 1935 musical for some time, but it was not until co-producers Martin Melcher and Joe Pasternak reactivated it as a vehicle for Day that the project was finally realized.

Originally staged by John Murray Anderson and George Abbott as the final production to play New York's legendary Hippodrome Theatre, *Jumbo* had been a commercial failure on the stage, running only five months despite the presence of Jimmy Durante and a cast of ninety, almost as many animals, and a plethora of extravagant production numbers. When MGM bought the rights to the show, its producer Billy Rose stipulated in the transaction that his name must be included in the official title of any subsequent film version.

Thus it was that, twenty-seven years after its Broadway premiere, *Billy Rose's Jumbo* came to the screen. Arriving as it did at the very end of the golden era of MGM musicals, *Jumbo* stands as a magnificent climax to one of the most vital film genres.

Sidney Sheldon's adaptation of Ben Hecht and Charles MacArthur's original book casts Doris Day as Kitty Wonder, bareback rider and trapeze artist of the Wonder Circus. Run somewhat haphazardly by Kitty's father (Jimmy Durante), who has a weakness for crap games, the Wonder Circus is constantly on the edge of bankruptcy. Their star attraction is the phenomenal Jumbo, a multitalented elephant who at once represents the circus' biggest financial and spiritual asset.

When Sam Rawlins (Stephen Boyd) joins the circus as a roustabout, the troupe's creditors begin to disappear. Kitty, whose transient life style has precluded any real possibilities for romance, falls in love with him. When Sam has proven almost indispensable to the welfare of the circus and the morale of its employees, Pop Wonder's major rival, John Noble (Dean Jagger), forecloses on the Wonder Circus. It seems that Sam is Noble's son, and by infiltrating the Wonder Circus, he has acquired all of its debts and signed them over to his father for collection.

THAT TOUCH OF MINK (1962).
With Cary Grant

BILLY ROSE'S JUMBO (1962). As Kitty Wonder

BILLY ROSE'S JUMBO (1962). With Martha Raye

Sam has also fallen in love with Kitty, however, and as the film ends, he is reunited with her, her father, and her stepmother Lulu (Martha Raye) as the four of them envision a bigger, better circus than ever before.

The elegiac mood that suffuses *Jumbo* operates on two levels. On an immediate level the film is dealing with the end of the circus as a viable force in American entertainment. On a deeper level, however, *Jumbo* is a twilight ode signaling the end of the American musical film. Everything is over in *Jumbo*. The joy and beauty of the musical numbers are tinged with a melancholy that deepens and enriches every viewing of this neglected masterpiece.

Charles Walters, who directed Day in *Please Don't Eat the Daisies*, is one of Hollywood's most underrated directors. His credits include such delightful musicals as *Good News, Easter Parade, The Barkleys of Broadway,* and *The Belle of New York. Billy Rose's Jumbo* is arguably his finest movie. Shot through with a nostalgia that never descends to cheap sentiment or camp, the movie has an insouciant and exhilarating energy that places it squarely among the very best film musicals.

This energy pervades every musical number in *Jumbo*. Working closely with his second unit director Busby Berkeley, Walters fashions the numbers with such care and precision that they flow naturally, build gradually, and eventually explode with a generosity that is heart-stopping. Walters is a master at correlating the movements of his camera with the cadences of a song and the motions of a dance.

For instance, the camera work that accompanies Day's exuberant singing of "This Can't Be Love" reflects the joy of Richard Rodgers' melody as well as the elation of the character. This union of camera movement with music receives its most sublime expression during Boyd's solo, "The Most Beautiful Girl in the World." The structure of this number resembles a short story within the larger framework of the movie itself.

Day is trying to repair the calliope whistle on the carousel. When Boyd offers to assist her, she rushes off to remove the grease from her face and returns in a lovely pink-and-white dress, hoping that he will notice her more feminine appearance. Boyd completes the repair work, and the calliope begins to play Rodgers' lilting waltz. Boyd starts to sing almost to himself while putting away his tools.

After finishing the song, Boyd

BILLY ROSE'S JUMBO (1962). With Stephen Boyd

*BILLY ROSE'S JUMBO (1962). With Martha Raye,
Jimmy Durante, and Dean Jagger*

begins to walk away as the music continues softly. Determined to be noticed, Day glides over to him and removes the tool box from his hands. As she moves toward him, the movement of the carousel and the music of the song infect her so that she starts waltzing without even realizing it. Setting his tools aside, she pauses and takes him in her arms. Walters cuts immediately to a vertiginous high-angle shot as the music crescendos and the couple dance ecstatically over the ground, communicating a feeling of euphoria that draws the viewer giddily into the rhythm of the music.

For sheer brilliance, however, nothing in *Jumbo* compares with its first number, "Over and Over Again." Beginning simply as Day sings to a young girl practicing on the trapeze, the theme of Hart's lyric, namely that "practice makes perfect," is developed in a series of tableaux depicting performers rehearsing on trampolines, seals balancing rubber balls, a somersaulting human ladder, and trapeze artists flying through the air. The number builds in momentum until its climax, when Walters captures the entire interior of the tent in a CinemaScope long shot, all three rings magically transformed into an area of whirling activity.

The musical pleasures in *Jumbo* are manifold. Day and Martha

120

Raye duet the plaintive "Why Can't I?" as they sit on the edge of their lantern-lit wagon, receding down a lonely stretch of country road. Day herself does full justice to two of Rodgers' loveliest ballads, "My Romance" and "Little Girl Blue." The latter is especially effective in Walters' use of the empty tent with its vast ring, his camera circling Day's isolated figure as she sings, the blue lights rotating around her forming a poignant visual counterpoint. And then there is the exultant finale, "Sawdust, Spangles and Dreams," in which Boyd jumps atop a ramshackle wagon, mesmerizing his audience of three with a straw hat and a spiel defining the circus as a world of illusion and half-forgotten memories.

In *Jumbo* Doris Day gives her one performance in a sixties movie that can hold its own with her best work of the fifties. The shrillness of her playing in the Shapiro comedies has vanished, and she looks lovelier than ever as well. Gone are the platinum wigs of her Universal vehicles; her hair in *Jumbo* is long and natural, the color of spun honey. Day subtly coordinates her entire body into one of the most total performances of her career. When she realizes that Boyd has been secretly undermining her father's circus, Walters shoots her

BILLY ROSE'S JUMBO (1962). The finale, with Martha Raye, Jimmy Durante, and Stephen Boyd

THE THRILL OF IT ALL (1963). With James Garner

reaction with her back to the camera. Her shoulders momentarily sag, but she pulls herself together, regains her posture, and moves quietly away without saying a word.

Not only does Day's performance carry the show, her character is also the emotional and moral center of the narrative. Although she is the star of the circus, she helps out wherever and whenever necessary. She is initially discovered scrubbing the back of a beautiful white horse. She takes time out from this chore to cajole and charm her father's creditors. When most of the troupe threaten to quit because Durante has gambled away their pay, Day rides into town and wins back the entire $800 her father had lost earlier in the day.

When she falls in love with Boyd, she refuses to wait for him to court her. She confides to Raye that she's not actually chasing him, just "stalking him a little." Ultimately, she even proposes to him. Thus, Kitty Wonder is a synthesis of the diverse elements that constitute the persona of Doris Day. She is at once a tomboy and a lady. Determined and aggressive when she is pursuing something that she wants, she remains vulnerable in her relationships with Boyd and Durante.

Walters gets persuasive performances from his entire cast. Martha Raye is marvelous as Lulu, the perennial good sport whose love for Durante is so enduring she even lets him shoot her out of a cannon. Durante himself is superb, and he repeats the moment that stopped the stage version. Caught red-handed trying to sneak Jumbo away from his creditors, Durante is asked where he thinks he's going with the elephant. With an incredulous look of innocence on his face, Durante replies, "What elephant?"

Even Stephen Boyd gives the most relaxed, charming performance of his career. Ultimately, however, the lion's share of honors must go to Charles Walters who created both a glorious valentine to the circus and a triumphant swan song for the movie musical.

Ironically, *Billy Rose's Jumbo* was the only one of Doris Day's films around this period that lost money. Its poor showing at the box office supposedly cost Day the lead in *The Unsinkable Molly Brown*, a project that Metro had been developing with her in mind.

The star recaptured her audience, however, with her next film, *The Thrill of it All*. Released in August of 1963, this product of the Universal glamour mill was the actress' third—and last—effort under the aegis of producer Ross Hunter. (He also produced *Pillow Talk* and *Midnight Lace*.) Day's husband Martin Melcher shared producing credit with Hunter.

THE THRILL OF IT ALL (1963). With Lillian Culver, Gertrude Flynn, and James Garner

The Thrill of it All has a bit more substance and bite than most of Day's comedies for Universal, primarily because Carl Reiner's screenplay is far superior to the marshmallow humor of Stanley Shapiro. Norman Jewison's lively direction is an added dividend. Jewison was just beginning his movie career, and he had not yet discovered the themes of social significance which would unfortunately turn him into a successor to Stanley Kramer.

Day lives in suburbia with her obstetrician husband James Garner and their two children. Invited to dinner at the home of the manufac-turer of Happy Soap, Day recounts an anecdote of how she got the children to use the soap. The septuagenarian tycoon (Reginald Owen) is so enchanted by her impromptu recitation that he persuades her to replace the Monroe-like "starling" who has been selling the soap on television.

Soon Day is earning $80,000 a year selling Happy Soap on the tube. Her burgeoning career puts a strain on her marriage, however, and when Garner rebels against her job, Reiner's script suddenly goes soft.

Garner tries to make Day jealous in the hope that she will forget Hap-

THE THRILL OF IT ALL (1963). With James Garner

py Soap and return to her household duties. He leaves photographs
of other women lying around,
smudges lipstick on his collar, becomes suddenly busy every night,
comes home drunk, and whispers
the names of strange women in his
sleep. Ultimately, Day opts for the
home and another baby. Content to
return to her place as a doctor's
wife, she obliterates all vestiges of
her independence by the final reel.

Before Reiner's cop-out ending,
The Thrill of it All offers more than
its share of merriment and wit.
Much of the satire directed at the
world of advertising and television
commercials is sharp and pointed,

far more pungent than Shapiro's
feeble thrusts at the same milieu in
Lover Come Back. Day's first appearance on television is hilarious.
She forgets her lines, hesitates and
stutters throughout the spot, and
her spiel is uncomfortably punc-
tuated with "uh's" and "well's."
Day does this bit really well; it
looks totally unrehearsed and yet
curiously persuasive in its own way.
Even though the studio technicians
snicker all the way through the
filming, twelve thousand people call
the station to voice their approval.
Day's persona proves eminently
more sympathetic to the potential
buyer of Happy Soap than that of

her sexpot predecessor.

Not surprisingly, Doris Day finds the idea of an independent career more stimulating than bottling catsup in her cellar or any of the other mundane duties she is expected to perform around the house. When Garner opposes the idea, Day remarks that attending the PTA is not her idea of self-fulfillment. For most of *The Thrill of it All*, Doris Day presents a portrait of the suburban housewife in rebellion. After she has so admirably asserted her right to self-realization, it is twice as distressing to see her let petty jealousy curtail her spirit, relegating her finally to domestic paralysis.

Most of Day's subsequent roles would find her increasingly entrenched in the suburbs, all avenues for escape by way of a productive, fulfilling career cut off forever. A loss of energy in the actress' performances parallels this trend in her roles; it's almost as though she has lost much of her enthusiasm for making movies.

Doris Day's second outing in 1963, *Move Over, Darling*, reunited her with James Garner as well as *Pillow Talk* director Michael Gordon. The plot of this purported comedy is as old as D. W. Griffith's *Enoch Arden*, a 1911 Biograph release. Based on a character in a poem by Alfred Lord Tennyson, Arden is a man who returns to his family after he has long been believed dead. This story has formed the basis for countless movies, most notably Garson Kanin's *My Favorite Wife* (1940).

Move Over, Darling is a direct remake of the Kanin film with Day in the Irene Dunne role, James Garner replacing Cary Grant, and Polly Bergen in the part originated by Gail Patrick. Day is the wife thought dead for five years who returns the very day her husband (Garner) has married his second wife (Polly Bergen). The suspension of belief necessary for such improbable farce to work is absent here. One keeps wondering why Garner doesn't just tell Bergen the truth. The inevitable mixups and misunderstandings are tasteless and unamusing. The jokes about Day's memorial service, which featured her favorite pink carnations, evoke embarrassment rather than laughter.

Director Gordon's heavy-handed execution of this delicate material sentimentalizes the characters and

THE IMAGE CONGEALS

precludes any opportunity for charm or humor. Gordon's visual style is even less imaginative in *Move Over, Darling* than it was in *Pillow Talk*. This time the flipover wipe replaces the split screen as Gordon's visual *piéce de résistance*. The flipover wipe is a television technique, an easy way to get from one scene to another by simultaneously wiping the image off the screen and turning the image itself inside out. This transition device appears with alarming frequency in Day's subsequent sixties films.

The actress has never been more abrasive than in *Move Over, Darling*. Her behavior actually seems regressive at times. When she becomes angry, she jumps up and down, stomps her feet, and stands square-toed with her fists clenched by her side, her platinum hair falling all over her face. (One wonders if she had access to an unlimited supply of peroxide on that desert island where she was stranded for five years). Day also tackles a Swedish accent in this movie when she impersonates a masseuse in order to prevent Garner from consummating his marriage to Bergen.

Move Over, Darling earned a tragic footnote in film history as the project on which Marilyn Monroe

MOVE OVER, DARLING (1963). With Thelma Ritter

had begun work when she committed suicide. The original title was *Something's Gotta Give*, its director was George Cukor, and the cast included, in addition to Monroe, Dean Martin and Cyd Charisse in the roles later played by James Garner and Polly Bergen. The facsimile of Cukor's home, which was reconstructed on the 20th Century-Fox sound stages for the Monroe film, was retained for use as Garner and Doris Day's house in *Move Over, Darling*.

Day's sole 1964 release found her once again working under director Norman Jewison but with less happy results than their previous collaboration on *The Thrill of it All*. *Send Me No Flowers* is yet another one-joke farce, deriving most of its dubious humor from the idea that Rock Hudson thinks he's dying of heart trouble. Hudson, a confirmed hypochondriac, overhears his doctor analyzing an older patient's cardiogram results and jumps to the conclusion that the terminal case under discussion is his own.

Send Me No Flowers was Day's third, and last, film co-starring Rock Hudson. One of the central problems with the movie is the difficulty one has in accepting Rock Hudson, a paradigm of the hale and hearty American male, as a whining hypochondriac. Watching this healthy specimen mewl and whimper as he swallows a pill every other minute puts a real strain on the credibility of the character.

Day herself is reasonably adequate as Hudson's indulgent but knowing wife (she makes his sleeping pills out of sugar), but the role itself is secondary to her male co-star. *Send Me No Flowers* typifies the growing tendency of Day's films to transplant her to suburbia. When the movie opens, she is preparing breakfast for Hudson. Dressed in a large bathrobe and fur houseshoes, she exchanges local gossip with the milkman, steps on an unappetizing amalgam of broken eggs and leaves, and gets her robe caught in the front door, eventually managing to lock herself out of the house. Day now moves with reluctant ease through a world circumscribed by station wagons and commuter trains. Jean Louis still designs her wardrobe, but the perimeters of her existence are defined by golf courses, tennis courts, and country clubs.

The actress appeared in only one movie in 1965. *Do Not Disturb* is little more than an inflated situation comedy, and a singularly unfunny one at that. Married to an executive in wool (Rod Taylor) who has been transferred to London by his firm, Day rents a country house in Kent instead of an apartment in the city. Taylor resents commuting, the menagerie of animals Day adopts, and the resemblance of his new home to a warehouse.

MOVE OVER, DARLING (1963). With Polly Bergen, Pat Harrington, Jr., and James Garner

*SEND ME NO FLOWERS (1964). A disastrous morning
for wife Judy*

When Day's landlady (Hermione Baddeley) sees Taylor dining in London with his lovely secretary (Maura McGiveney), she decides to help her tenant arouse Taylor's jealousy. Baddeley introduces Day to Sergio Fantoni, an urbane antiques dealer. Fantoni flies Day to Paris to see a Georgian dining room set he has for sale in his shop there. (She desperately wants to buy such a set for her forthcoming anniversary.) The predictable complications ensue when the actress gets crocked on French champagne, misses the last airplane back to London, and winds up spending the night with Fantoni in the window of his store.

Doris Day's collision with Continental culture would make Henry James blanch. She has trouble learning the money in London. She is unable to remember on which side of the road to drive. She aborts a fox hunt by hiding the fox from the hunters and protecting it from the dogs. When she hits Paris, one could swear that a hint of self-parody has crept into *Do Not Disturb*. A group of French children asks her if she knows Rock Hudson or Daniel Boone. When each child lines up to share his wine with her, Day is surprised to discover the drink is not a Coca-Cola. Recognizing the actress' proclivity toward alcohol, the movie has her get so drunk that she replaces a one-man band in a tavern, lustily sings a risqué *chanson*, and enthusiastically joins a soccer game in the street. What Day's extended drunk scene lacks in subtlety, it makes up for in gusto and fervor. The high-pitched squeals and giggles that indicate the actress' elation in many of her later performances are especially grating during this sequence.

The star's 1966 entry, *The Glass Bottom Boat*, is the first of two movies Doris Day appeared in under the direction of Frank Tashlin. Tashlin joins Alfred Hitchcock and Stanley Donen as one of the three best directors under whom the actress has worked. Although neither *The Glass Bottom Boat* nor their subsequent collaboration *Caprice* (1967) are among Tashlin's best movies, they are decidedly superior to the indistinguishable comedies Day had been churning out during the sixties.

Along with Preston Sturges, Frank Tashlin is one of the great satirists in the American cinema. No other director has so relentlessly and so merrily attacked the absurdities of modern life. In *The Glass Bottom Boat*, Tashlin's targets are, in no particular order, NASA, government bureaucracy, the CIA, James Bond, tourism, and space-age technology.

Doris Day again plays a widow (with no children) who doubles as a tour guide for a space research complex and a mermaid for tour-

SEND ME NO FLOWERS (1964). With Tony Randall and Rock Hudson

ists to ogle from her father's glass-bottom boat. Day finds herself once more the victim of male duplicity when research scientist Rod Taylor eyes her giving tours. He hires her to be his biographer while he develops the non-existent Project Venus, a ruse he has concocted to expedite his seduction of the unsuspecting Day.

The numerous "bugs" planted throughout the space center conclude that Day is a Russian agent, ingratiating herself with Taylor in order to obtain top security information. The blunders that ensue

give director Tashlin free rein for his special brand of anarchic humor.

Tashlin satirizes everything in *The Glass Bottom Boat*, even the romance between Taylor and Day. When Day realizes she is falling in love with the scientist, Tashlin films her sentimental love song in the synthetic style of slick romantic movies, both commenting on the artifice and reveling in it.

Originating his career with the direction of "Looneytoons" and "Merrie Melodies," this former cartoonist brought to his feature

DO NOT DISTURB (1965). With Rod Taylor

THE GLASS BOTTOM BOAT (1966). With Dom De Luise

films the style and contours of the animated short. Inanimate objects, especially bizarre gadgets devised for modern convenience, assume lives of their own in *The Glass Bottom Boat*. For example, the supposedly labor-saving utensils in Rod Taylor's kitchen reduce the room to a microcosm of chaos and anarchy. When Doris Day tries to bake a cake in the oven, she winds up under siege from an automatic floor-cleaner, its obscenely-shaped funnel literally crawling up her blouse. Similarly, her inability to command Taylor's runaway remote-control speedboat illustrates the difficulty of human control over such independent mechanisms.

Individual set pieces, such as Day and Dom De Luise encounter with a banana cream cake in an empty pail and Paul Lynde's drag routine, are truly hilarious, but *The Glass Bottom Boat* lacks the consistent brilliance of Tashlin's best movies, specifically *Artists and Models* and *The Girl Can't Help It*. The film's primary weakness is its diffused

THE GLASS BOTTOM BOAT (1966). With Rod Taylor

CAPRICE (1967). As Patricia Fowler

CAPRICE (1967). With Richard Harris

THE BALLAD OF JOSIE (1968). With John Fiedler and Peter Graves

structure. The grotesqueries Tashlin usually embodies in one person, such as Jerry Lewis or Jayne Mansfield, are scattered among several characters. No matter how gamely Day, Dom De Luise, Paul Lynde, and Dick Martin try, their combined effort is small compensation for the absence of one Jerry Lewis.

Day acquits herself admirably while she undergoes an unusual amount of physically strenuous comedy. Her natural athleticism has never been better utilized than under Tashlin. Her performance in general is capable enough, but the part itself is atypical of her vehicles around this time in that it requires Day to fit into an ensemble rather than dominate the proceedings.

Frank Tashlin's distress over the growing dichotomy between the natural and the synthetic receives its most pessimistic expression in *Caprice*. Doris Day herself becomes the director's central metaphor for the synthetic nature of society. Day's first appearance in

THE BALLAD OF JOSIE (1968). In the title role

WHERE WERE YOU WHEN THE LIGHTS WENT OUT? (1968).
With Robert Morse

Caprice is a grotesque exaggeration of her mid-sixties image. She lowers the newspaper she is reading to reveal a platinum-haired mannequin with enormous dark glasses where her eyes should be. She is a walking advertisement for vinyl in her black-and-white checkered coat, gold dress and hat, matching gold handbag, and black mesh stockings topped by high gold boots. Day's wax-like makeup completes the image of an artifact exhumed for public display.

Tashlin frames this exploration of Day's calcified image amid a swirling background of duplicity and mendacity in the cosmetics industry. Day plays Patricia Fowler, an industrial designer whose father, an Interpol agent, is slain in Switzerland as the film opens. Day shuttles between two international cosmetics firms, spying on each of them in turn until she uncovers the network of drug agents responsible for her father's death. (It seems her father had discovered that a newly invented face powder was transformed into a powerful hallucinogen when burned, its ashes providing the source of income for an international conspircacy of criminal contrabandists).

The kaleidoscopic narrative gives Tashlin ample opportunity for some lacerating assaults against the artifice in the world of cosmetics. The most deadly espionage tactics are employed to steal formulae for underarm roll-on deodorants and water-repellent hair sprays. *Caprice* may be the director's darkest exploration of the anesthetization of contemporary life, but Tashlin's satire is never motivated by hate. Endlessly amused by the artifice of this society and the twin components of success and illusion which nurture it, Tashlin enjoys every absurdity, every perversion, and gleefully incorporates his enjoyment into the mainstream of his attacks.

Tashlin's love of gadgets and gimmicks is in full evidence in *Caprice*. When Day discovers that every item on the table where she is eating with Richard Harris is bugged, she bursts the eavesdroppers' eardrums by munching potato chips, burping, downing

WITH SIX YOU GET EGGROLL (1968). With Brian Keith

On her television show with Kaye Ballard (1972)

Alka Seltzer, hitting her silverware against a glass, and stirring the sugar cubes in her coffee cup with extraordinary vigor. Tashlin also ridicules the effects of mass media upon human sensibilities. When Day and Harris escape from some pursuers by crawling through the window of an apartment, the children watching television do not even notice the interruption.

Tashlin can also laugh at himself, however. At one point Day goes to the movies during the course of an assignment, and the film she sits down to watch is—*Caprice*, starring Doris Day.

The actress has never had a role that required so much physical exertion. She falls out of the balcony of a movie theater, dangles from precipices, slides down mountainsides, and is repeatedly shot at during an excitingly filmed ski chase. She is still the indomitable heroine, however, who lets nothing deter her in the search for her father's murderer. Through the single-mindedness of her quest, Patricia Fowler emerges as the logical extension of Doris Day's persona in the mid-sixties: determined, independent, and, in the midst of the artificiality and mechanization surrounding her, irrevocably true to herself.

In 1968 Doris Day appeared in the last three movies of her career to date. The first of these, *The Ballad of Josie*, is rather interesting for the changes it rings on Day's persona as well as its overt women's lib theme. Day is a widow again, living in Wyoming territory, who wants to turn her 480 acres of land into a profit-making enterprise. Dissuaded by cattle rancher Peter Graves from raising cows, she uses her acres to start a sheep ranch, thus precipitating the traditional conflict between cattlemen and sheepherders. Day fights the cattlemen in a manner reminiscent of her battle against the railroad in *It Happened to Jane*, but when she realizes her persistence will end in bloodshed, she offers to relinquish her flock.

Impressed by her stamina and determination, Day's nemesis George Kennedy offers to purchase her flock of sheep, a transaction which will give her enough revenue to buy some good cattle and bulls. In a way she has won her point; but her victory is somewhat mitigated when the exigencies of the plot require her to burn her men's duds in the fireplace and marry Graves in the final reel.

The impression of Doris Day's Josie Minick that lingers in the memory, however, is one of a genuine "right-on" frontier woman. The following tirade she delivers to the cattlemen who are trying to interfere with the raising of her sheep is a worthy expostulation on the basic tenets of women's lib:

"Forget I'm a woman. I'm a human being. I can take care of myself and my son without anybody's charity. I can think and I can work . . . . I don't want a man, and I don't need a man. I've got myself and I've got my sheep, and I'm gonna bring 'em through to spring, and I'm gonna sell my lambs and my wool, and I'm gonna double my money—and *nobody* . . . nobody, not a damn one of you, is gonna get in my way."

Day's subsequent movies in 1968 are neither as absorbing nor as engaging as *The Ballad of Josie. Where Were You When the Lights Went Out?* is undoubtedly the worst film of her career. Set against the New York blackout of 1965, the movie merely uses that emergency as a jumping point for a tired farce, most of which occurs in the suburbs of Connecticut. Day plays a married stage actress who, trying to strike back at the infidelity of her husband (Patrick O'Neal) on the night of the blackout, becomes in-

On television

nocently involved with a harried young embezzler (Robert Morse).

Day's final movie thus far in her career, *With Six You Get Eggroll*, has all the earmarks of a pilot for her succeeding television series. Playing a widow with three boys who runs her late husband's construction business, Day is reintroduced by her matchmaking sister Pat Carroll to an old acquaintance, chemical engineer Brian Keith. They date, fall in love, and marry—much to the chagrin of their respective offspring.

Although its television underpinnings are never completely dispelled, *With Six You Get Eggroll* presents a refreshing portrait of Doris Day as a middle-aged woman who accepts her age with equanimity (her oldest son in the film is in his late teens) and responds with real passion to Keith's romantic overtures. The quality of their relationship is intensified by the rapport Day and Keith evince in their scenes together. Unlike many of the star's preceding comedies, male and female are on equal footing with one another in *With Six You Get Eggroll*.

Before the release of *Where Were You When the Lights Went Out?*, Martin Melcher consolidated, in *Variety*'s words, "one of the industry's all-time plush talent deals" when he finalized a contract with CBS for a television series starring his wife. Day was to play a young widow who lives on a ranch with her two children. Before filming began on the series, however, Melcher died of bacterial endocarditis, an infection of the heart muscle. It is a tribute to Doris Day's stamina and professionalism that six weeks after her husband's death, she was filming the initial segment of the series Melcher had arranged for her.

"The Doris Day Show" was an immediate success and continued on the air for several years, surviving various alterations of character, locale, and format. Since the series ended, the actress has devoted most of her time and energy to her favorite charity, Actors for Animals. She has also done extensive work combating the growing problem of air pollution.

In 1974 Doris Day won a $22 million judgment from an attorney accused of defrauding her over a period of many years. The star's last public appearance was on a CBS-TV special in February, 1975.

One hopes that Doris Day's continued absence from the screen will not be permanent. She has amply demonstrated in the past that she has the dramatic skill necessary to tackle the most challenging kind of role—and succeed triumphantly. Much of her most creative work might still lie ahead.

What she *has* contributed to the movies so far is sufficient to insure her a niche in the annals of screen history. Her lengthy career is endlessly fascinating in that her failures as well as her many successes reveal facets of a persona that was never stationary but continually evolving over a period of twenty years. She brought genuine gaiety and enthusiasm to the musicals in which she appeared. She brought unexpected resonance to such atypical, demanding roles as Ruth Etting in *Love Me or Leave Me* and Jo McKenna in *The Man Who Knew Too Much*. Ultimately, in those movies where her work was central to her role, she embodied the free-willed, free-spirited modern female who renounces domesticity and docile subservience to a male. She was the most forward-looking heroine in American movies for two decades. In resisting the attempts of so many of her later films to institutionalize her genuine, natural talents, Doris Day remained true to herself in a manner that defines her as a star of the highest magnitude.

BIBLIOGRAPHY

Cameron, Ian. "Hitchcock and the Mechanics of Suspense."
———. "Hitchcock: Suspense and Meaning."
———. "Frank Tashlin and the New World." *Movie Reader*. New York: Praeger, 1972.
Candee, Marjorie Dent (ed.). *Current Biography*. New York: The H.W. Wilson Co., 1954.
Davidson, Bill. "The Change in Doris Day." *TV Guide*, February 20, 1971.
Gardella, Kay. "Doris Day Returns with a 'Now' Look in Her TV Special." *New York Sunday News*, February 16, 1975.
Hallowell, John. "Will the Real Doris Day Sing Out." *The New York Times*, October 27, 1968.
Haskell, Molly. *From Reverence to Rape: The Treatment of Women in the Movies*. New York: Holt, Rinehart and Winston, Inc., 1974.
Kobal, John. *Gotta Sing, Gotta Dance*. London: The Hamlyn Publishing Group Ltd., 1970.
McVay, Douglas. *The Musical Film*. New York: A.S. Barnes & Co., 1967.
Michael, Paul. *The American Movies Reference Book: The Sound Era*. Englewood Cliffs, N.J.: Prentice-Hall, Inc., 1969.
Sarris, Andrew. *The American Cinema*. New York: E.P. Dutton & Co., Inc., 1968.
Shipman, David. *The Great Movie Stars: The International Years*. New York: St. Martin's Press, Inc., 1972.
Vallance, Tom. *The American Musical*. New York: A.S. Barnes & Co., 1970.
Wasserman, John L. "I Don't Even Like Apple Pie." *TV Guide*, December 6, 1969.
Whitburn, Joel. *Top Pop Records, 1955-1970*. Detroit: Gale Research Company, 1972.
Whitney, Dwight. "All Sugar, No Spice." *TV Guide*, December 28, 1968.

THE FILMS OF DORIS DAY

The director's name follows the release date. A (c) following the release date indicates that the film is in color. Sp indicates screenplay and b/o indicates based on.

1. ROMANCE ON THE HIGH SEAS. Warner Bros., 1948. (c) *Michael Curtiz*. Sp: Julius J. and Philip G. Epstein, b/o story by S. Pondal Rios and Carlos A. Olivari. Cast: Jack Carson, Janis Paige, Don DeFore, Oscar Levant, S.Z. Sakall, Fortunio Bonanova, Eric Blore, Franklin Pangborn, Avon Long.

2. MY DREAM IS YOURS. Warner Bros., 1949. (c) *Michael Curtiz*. Sp: Harry Kurnitz and Dane Lussier. Cast: Jack Carson, Lee Bowman, Adolphe Menjou, Eve Arden, S.Z. Sakall, Selena Royle, Edgar Kennedy, Franklin Pangborn.

3. IT'S A GREAT FEELING. Warner Bros., 1949. (c) *David Butler*. Sp: Jack Rose and Mel Shavelson, b/o story by I.A.L. Diamond. Cast: Dennis Morgan, Jack Carson, Bill Goodwin, Gary Cooper, Joan Crawford, Sydney Greenstreet, Danny Kaye, Patricia Neal, Eleanor Parker, Ronald Reagan, Edward G. Robinson, Jane Wyman.

4. YOUNG MAN WITH A HORN. Warner Bros., 1950. *Michael Curtiz*. Sp: Carl Foreman and Edmund H. North, b/o novel by Dorothy Baker. Cast: Kirk Douglas, Lauren Bacall, Hoagy Carmichael, Juano Hernandez, Jerome Cowan, Mary Beth Hughes.

5. TEA FOR TWO. Warner Bros., 1950. (c) *David Butler*. Sp: Harry Clork, b/o play by Frank Mandel, Otto Harbach, Vincent Youmans, and Emil Nyitray. Cast: Gordon MacRae, Gene Nelson, Patrice Wymore, Eve Arden, Billy De Wolfe, S.Z. Sakall, Bill Goodwin. Previously filmed in 1930 and 1940 as *No, No, Nanette*.

6. THE WEST POINT STORY. Warner Bros., 1950. *Roy Del Ruth*. Sp: John Monks, Jr., Charles Hoffman, and Irving Wallace, b/o story by Wallace. Cast: James Cagney, Virginia Mayo, Gordon MacRae, Gene Nelson, Alan Hale, Jr., Roland Winters, Jerome Cowan.

7. STORM WARNING. Warner Bros., 1951. *Stuart Heisler*. Sp: Daniel Fuchs and Richard Brooks. Cast: Ginger Rogers, Ronald Reagan, Steve Cochran, Hugh Sanders, Lloyd Gough, Raymond Greenleaf.

8. LULLABY OF BROADWAY. Warner Bros., 1951. (c) *David Butler*. Sp: Earl Baldwin. Cast: Gene Nelson, S.Z. Sakall, Billy De Wolfe, Gladys George, Florence Bates.

9. ON MOONLIGHT BAY. Warner Bros., 1951. (c) *Roy Del Ruth*. Sp: Jack Rose and Melville Shavelson, b/o stories by Booth Tarkington. Cast: Gordon MacRae, Jack Smith, Leon Ames, Rosemary De Camp, Mary Wickes, Ellen Corby, Billy Gray.

10. STARLIFT. Warner Bros., 1951. *Roy Del Ruth*. Sp: John Klorer and Karl Kamb, b/o story by Klorer. Cast: Gordon MacRae, Virginia Mayo, Gene Nelson, Ruth Roman, Janice Rule, Dick Wesson, Ron Hagerthy, James Cagney, Gary Cooper, Phil Harris, Frank Lovejoy, Louella Parsons, Randolph Scott, Jane Wyman, Patrice Wymore.

11. I'LL SEE YOU IN MY DREAMS. Warner Bros., 1952. *Michael Curtiz*. Sp: Melville Shavelson and Jack Rose. Cast: Danny Thomas, Frank Lovejoy, Patrice Wymore, James Gleason, Mary Wickes, Jim Backus, Minna Gombell.

12. THE WINNING TEAM. Warner Bros., 1952. *Lewis Seiler*. Sp: Ted Sherdeman, Seeleg Lester, and Merwin Gerard, b/o story by Lester and Gerard. Cast: Ronald Reagan, Frank Lovejoy, Eve Miller, James Millican, Rusty Tamblyn, Gordon Jones, Hugh Sanders.

13. APRIL IN PARIS. Warner Bros., 1953. (c) *David Butler*. Sp: Jack Rose and Melville Shavelson. Cast: Ray Bolger, Claude Dauphin, Eve Miller, George Givot, Paul Harvey.

14. BY THE LIGHT OF THE SILVERY MOON. Warner Bros., 1953. (c) *David Butler*. Sp: Robert O'Brien and Irving Elinson, b/o stories by Booth Tarkington. Cast: Gordon MacRae, Leon Ames, Rosemary De Camp, Billy Gray, Mary Wickes, Russell Arms, Maria Palmer.

15. CALAMITY JANE. Warner Bros., 1953. (c) *David Butler*. Sp: James O'Hanlon. Cast: Howard Keel, Allyn McLerie, Philip Carey, Dick Wesson, Paul Harvey, Chubby Johnson, Gale Robbins.

16. LUCKY ME. Warner Bros., 1954. (c) *Jack Donohue*. Sp: James O'Hanlon, Robert O'Brien, and Irving Elinson, b/o story by O'Hanlon. Cast: Robert Cummings, Phil Silvers, Eddie Foy, Jr., Nancy Walker, Martha Hyer, Bill Goodwin, Marcel Dalio, Hayden Rorke.

17. YOUNG AT HEART. Warner Bros., 1954. (c) *Gordon Douglas*. Sp: Julius J. Epstein and Lenore Coffee, b/o story by Fannie Hurst. Cast: Frank Sinatra, Gig Young, Ethel Barrymore, Dorothy Malone, Elizabeth Fraser, Robert Keith, Alan Hale, Jr., Lonny Chapman. Previously filmed in 1938 as *Four Daughters*.

18. LOVE ME OR LEAVE ME. MGM, 1955. (c) *Charles Vidor*. Sp: Daniel Fuchs and Isobel Lennart, b/o story by Fuchs. Cast: James Cagney, Cameron Mitchell, Robert Keith, Tom Tully, Harry Bellaver.

19. THE MAN WHO KNEW TOO MUCH. Paramount, 1956. (c) *Alfred Hitchcock*. Sp: John Michael Hayes, b/o story by Charles Bennett and D.B. Wyndham-Lewis. Cast: James Stewart, Brenda de Banzie, Bernard Miles, Daniel Gelin, Christopher Olsen, Ralph Truman, Mogens Wieth. Previously filmed in 1934.

20. JULIE. MGM, 1956. *Andrew L. Stone*. Sp: Stone. Cast: Louis Jourdan, Barry Sullivan, Frank Lovejoy, John Gallaudet, Harlan Warde, Jack Kruschen.

21. PAJAMA GAME. Warner Bros., 1957. (c) *George Abbott and Stanley Donen*. Sp: Abbott and Richard Bissell, b/o play by Abbott and Bissell. Cast: John Raitt, Carol Haney, Eddie Foy, Jr., Reta Shaw, Barbara Nichols, Thelma Pelish, Jack Straw, Ralph Dunn.

22. TEACHER'S PET. Paramount, 1958. *George Seaton*. Sp: Fay and Michael Kanin. Cast: Clark Gable, Gig Young, Mamie Van Doren, Nick Adams, Peter Baldwin, Marion Ross, Jack Albertson.

23. TUNNEL OF LOVE. MGM, 1958. *Gene Kelly*. Sp: Joseph Fields, b/o play by Fields and Peter De Vries. Cast: Richard Widmark, Gig Young, Gia Scala, Elizabeth Fraser, Elizabeth Wilson, Vikki Dougan.

24. IT HAPPENED TO JANE. Columbia, 1959. (c) *Richard Quine*. Sp: Norman Katkov, b/o story by Katkov and Max Wilk. Cast: Jack Lemmon, Ernie Kovacs, Steve Forrest, Mary Wickes, Russ Brown.

25. PILLOW TALK. Universal, 1959. (c) *Michael Gordon*. Sp: Stanley Shapiro and Maurice Richlin, b/o story by Russell Rouse and Clarence Greene. Cast: Rock Hudson, Tony Randall, Thelma Ritter, Nick Adams, Julia Meade, Allen Jenkins, Marcel Dalio, Lee Patrick.

26. PLEASE DON'T EAT THE DAISIES. MGM, 1960. (c) *Charles Walters*. Sp: Isobel Lennart, b/o book by Jean Kerr. Cast: David Niven, Janis Paige, Spring Byington, Richard Haydn, Patsy Kelly, Jack Weston, Carmen Phillips.

27. MIDNIGHT LACE. Universal, 1960. (c) *David Miller*. Sp: Ivan Goff and Ben Roberts, b/o play by Janet Green. Cast: Rex Harrison, John Gavin, Myrna Loy, Roddy McDowall, Herbert Marshall, Natasha Parry, Hermione Baddeley, John Williams, Richard Ney, Doris Lloyd.

28. LOVER COME BACK. Universal, 1961. (c) *Delbert Mann*. Sp: Stanley Shapiro and Paul Henning. Cast: Rock Hudson, Tony Randall, Edie Adams, Jack Oakie, Jack Kruschen, Ann B. Davis.

29. THAT TOUCH OF MINK. Universal, 1962. (c) *Delbert Mann*. Sp: Stanley Shapiro and Nate Monaster. Cast: Cary Grant, Gig Young, Audrey Meadows, Alan Hewitt, John Astin, Mickey Mantle, Roger Maris, Yogi Berra.

30. BILLY ROSE'S JUMBO. MGM, 1962. (c) *Charles Walters*. Sp: Sidney Sheldon, b/o play by Ben Hecht and Charles MacArthur. Cast: Stephen Boyd, Jimmy Durante, Martha Raye, Dean Jagger, Robert Burton, Grady Sutton.

31. THE THRILL OF IT ALL. Universal, 1963. (c) *Norman Jewison*. Sp: Carl Reiner, b/o story by Reiner and Larry Gelbart, Cast: James Garner, Arlene Francis, Edward Andrews, Reginald Owen, ZaSu Pitts, Elliott Reid, Alice Pearce.

32. MOVE OVER, DARLING. 20th Century-Fox, 1963. (c) *Michael Gordon*. Sp: Hal Kanter and Jack Sher, b/o screenplay by Bella and Samuel Spewack. Cast: James Garner, Polly Bergen, Chuck Connors, Thelma Ritter, Fred Clark, Don Knotts, Elliott Reid, Edgar Buchanan. Previously filmed in 1940 as *My Favorite Wife*.

33. SEND ME NO FLOWERS. Universal, 1964. (c) *Norman Jewison*. Sp: Julius Epstein, b/o play by Norman Barasch and Carroll Moore. Cast: Rock Hudson, Tony Randall, Clint Walker, Paul Lynde, Hal March, Edward Andrews, Patricia Barry.

34. DO NOT DISTURB. 20th Century-Fox, 1965. (c) *Ralph Levy*. Sp: Milt Rosen and Richard Breen, b/o play by William Fairchild. Cast: Rod Taylor, Hermione Baddeley, Sergio Fantoni, Reginald Gardiner, Maura McGiveney.

35. THE GLASS BOTTOM BOAT. MGM, 1966. (C) *Frank Tashlin*. Sp: Everett Freeman. Cast: Rod Taylor, Arthur Godfrey, John McGiver, Paul Lynde, Edward Andrews, Eric Fleming, Dom De Luise, Dick Martin, Elizabeth Fraser, Alice Pearce, Ellen Corby, George Tobias.

36. CAPRICE. 20th Century-Fox, 1967. (c) *Frank Tashlin*. Sp: Tashlin and Jay Jayson, b/o story by Jayson and Martin Hale. Cast: Richard Harris, Ray Walston, Jack Kruschen, Edward Mulhare, Lilia Skala, Michael J. Pollard.

37. THE BALLAD OF JOSIE. Universal, 1968. (c) *Andrew V. McLaglen*. Sp: Harold Swanton. Cast: Peter Graves, George Kennedy, Andy Devine, William Talman, David Hartman, Guy Raymond, Audrey Christie, Elizabeth Fraser, Don Stroud, Robert Lowery.

38. WHERE WERE YOU WHEN THE LIGHTS WENT OUT? MGM, 1968. (c) *Hy Averback*. Sp: Everett Freeman and Karl Tunberg, b/o play by Claude Magnier. Cast: Robert Morse, Terry-Thomas, Patrick O'Neal, Lola Albright, Steve Allen, Jim Backus, Ben Blue.

39. WITH SIX YOU GET EGGROLL. An Arwin Film Production, released by National General Pictures, 1968. (c) *Howard Morris*. Sp: Gwen Bagni, Paul Dubov, Harvey Bullock, and R.S. Allen, b/o story by Bagni and Dubov. Cast: Brian Keith, Pat Carroll, Barbara Hershey, George Carlin, Alice Ghostley, John Findlater, Jimmy Bracken, Richard Steele.

INDEX

155

ABOUT THE AUTHOR

George Morris graduated from the University of Texas in 1967 with a Bachelor of Fine Arts degree. He is the author of *Errol Flynn*, a volume in the Pyramid Illustrated History of the Movies and has contributed film criticism frequently to *The Village Voice* and *The Real Paper*. He has also written articles for *Film Comment*, *The Soho Weekly News*, *Changes*, and *Take One*.

ABOUT THE EDITOR

Ted Sennett is the author of *Warner Brothers Presents*, a tribute to the great Warners films of the thirties and forties, and of *Lunatics and Lovers*, on the long-vanished but well-remembered movie "screwball" comedies of the past. He is also the editor of *The Movie Buff's Book* and has written about films for magazines and newspapers. He lives in New Jersey with his wife and three children.